THE REMINISCENCES OF
Vice Admiral Truman J. Hedding
U.S. Navy (Retired)

INTERVIEWED BY
Etta Belle Kitchen

U.S. Naval Institute • Annapolis, Maryland

Copyright © 1972/1995

Preface--1972

This Manuscript is the result of several taped interviews with Vice Admiral Truman J. Hedding at his home in Coronado, California during a period from February to May 1971. These interviews were conducted by Commander Etta Belle Kitchen, USN (Retired) for the Oral History Office in the U. S. Naval Institute.

Only minor emendations have been made to the transcript by Admiral Hedding and so the reader is asked to bear in mind the fact that he is reading a transcript of the spoken word rather than the written word.

An index is affixed to the text for the greater convenience of the reader.

Dr. John T. Mason, Jr.

Preface--1995

The oral history transcript of Vice Admiral Hedding was one of the first to be published by the Naval Institute. As a result, some of the refinements that have later become standard parts of the format were not yet incorporated. This revised transcript has been annotated with footnotes to provide additional information, and the volume has been indexed in the comprehensive format now standard for Naval Institute oral history. In addition to the corrections made originally by Admiral Hedding, some slight editing has been done in the interest of clarity and smoothness. The original version of the transcript is still on file at the Naval Institute.

Paul Stillwell

VICE ADMIRAL TRUMAN J. HEDDING
UNITED STATES NAVY (RETIRED)

Truman Johnson Hedding was born on 14 July 1902 in Morrisdale, Pennsylvania, son of Dr. Benjamin E. Hedding and Mrs. Katherine C. Hedding. He attended East Denver High School and Denver (Colorado) University for one year before his appointment to the U.S. Naval Academy, Annapolis, Maryland, by the Honorable B. C. Hernandez of New Mexico in 1920. Graduated and commissioned ensign on 4 June 1924, he advanced to the rank of captain, his date of rank 1 June 1943. His nomination to the rank of rear admiral was confirmed by the Senate to date from 1 July 1951.

Following graduation from the Naval Academy in 1924, he served on board the USS Maryland (BB-46) until January 1925, when he was ordered to the Naval Air Station, Pensacola, Florida, for flight training. He was designated a naval aviator on 24 November 1926. He remained at the air station until 27 January 1927, when he was assigned to Fighting Squadron One, of Aircraft Squadrons Battle Fleet. From June 1929 to May 1930 he received instruction in aeronautical engineering at the Postgraduate School, Annapolis, and continued instruction at the Massachusetts Institute of Technology at Cambridge, from which he received the master of science degree in 1931.

Between July 1931 and June 1932 he was on duty at the Naval Air Station, Anacostia, D.C., after which he had a year's service in the USS Saratoga (CV-3). Assigned to Fighting Squadron Six-B until June 1935, he was next ordered to Washington, D.C., to serve in the Bureau of Aeronautics, Navy Department, with additional duty during 1936-37 as a naval aide to the White House. In June 1937 he joined Fighting Squadron Two-B, based on the USS Lexington (CV-2), and in December 1939 assumed command of Fighting Squadron Two on board that carrier. Following duty from June 1940 until June 1942 at the Naval Air Station, Pensacola, he assisted in fitting out the USS Essex (CV-9). From her commissioning, 31 December 1942, until July 1943, he had consecutive duty as air officer and executive officer.

In August 1943 he became chief of staff to Commander Carrier Division Three, and for outstanding service in that capacity was awarded the Legion of Merit and a letter of commendation, each with combat V. The citations follow in part:

Legion of Merit: "For exceptionally meritorious conduct . . . during successful attacks on enemy Japanese-held territory of Tarawa, Apamama, Makin, Jaluit, Wotje, Kwajalein, Truk, the Marianas, Palau, and Hollandia, from November 1943 to April 1944, and in the Naval Battle for the Marianas in June 1944 . . . Captain Hedding ably assisted the Task Force Commander in planning operations and in coordinating and directing attacks against hostile aircraft, shipping and shore installations. . . . He was greatly instrumental in forming plans which, when placed in effect by the units of the Task Force, caused great destruction on the enemy with little damage to our forces. . . ."

Letter of Commendation (by Commander in Chief Pacific Fleet): "For meritorious conduct . . . as Chief of Staff to the Task Force Commander during successful attacks on the Japanese-held islands of Tarawa, Apamama, Makin, Mille, Jaluit, Wotje and Kwajalein. His initiative and ability were outstanding in the execution of attacks against Tarawa, Makin and Apamama on 18 September 1943. During the period 10 to 25 November 1943, his exceptional performance of duty throughout offensive operations against the enemy contributed immeasurably to the destruction of enemy aircraft, shipping and installations at Mille, Makin and Jaluit. . ."

From June 1944 to March 1946 he served on the staff of the Commander in Chief Pacific Fleet, and for meritorious service in the Future Plans Section, concerned with naval and naval air operations, he was awarded the Bronze Star Medal. The citation states in part: "Captain Hedding ably discharged his responsibility for the planning of Carrier Task Force Operations against the Japanese Home Islands and the enemy-held positions." He is also entitled to the ribbon and stars for, and facsimiles of the Presidential Unit Citations awarded the USS Yorktown (CV-10), USS Lexington (CV-16), and USS Essex (CV-9).

Completing a tour of duty in March 1947 at the Naval Air Base, Fourteenth Naval District, Pearl Harbor, T.H., he returned to the Untied States and was assigned to the General Board, Navy Department, Washington, D.C. In August 1947 he reported for instruction at the National War College, also in Washington, and upon graduation assumed command of the USS Valley Forge (CV-45) in July 1948. Detached from that command in August 1949, he was ordered to the Joint Staff, Office of the Joint Chiefs of Staff, Washington. In April 1951 he joined the staff of the Commander in Chief Pacific Fleet, assuming the duty of Chief of Staff, Joint Staff, in August of that year.

In July 1953 he became Commander Formosa Patrol Force, Pacific Fleet, with additional duty as Commander Fleet Air Wing One. On 17 August 1954 he reported as

Deputy Director, Joint Strategic Plans Group, Joint Staff Office, Joint Chiefs of Staff, Washington, D.C. On 28 June 1955 he assumed the duty of Special Assistant to the Chairman of the Joint Chiefs of Staff. He was Commander Carrier Division Three from September 1957 until September 1957. On 14 October 1957 he reported as Bureau of Aeronautics general representative, Western District, with headquarters in Los Angeles, California. He remained there until relieved of all active duty pending his retirement, effective 1 January 1959. Upon being transferred to the retired list, he was advanced to the rank of vice admiral on the basis of combat awards.

In addition to the Legion of Merit with combat V, the Bronze Star medal, Commendation Ribbon with combat V, and the Presidential Unit Citation with three stars, Vice Admiral Hedding has the American Defense Service Medal; the American Campaign Medal; the Asiatic-Pacific Campaign Medal; World War II Victory Medal; and National Defense Service Medal. He married the former Miss Ysabel Weyse of Santa Monica, California.

DECLARATION OF TRUST

The undersigned does hereby appoint and designate as his (her) Trustee herein, the Secretary-Treasurer and Publisher of the United States Naval Institute to perform and discharge the following duties, powers, and privileges in connection with the possession and use of a certain taped interview between the undersigned and the Oral History Department of the United States Naval Institute.

1. Classification of Transcript.

(X)a. If classified OPEN, the transcript(s) may be read or the recording(s) audited by the qualified personnel upon presentation of proper credentials, as determined by the Secretary-Treasurer of the U. S. Naval Institute.

( )b. If classified PERMISSION REQUIRED TO CITE OR QUOTE, the user will be required to obtain permission in writing from the interviewee prior to quoting or citing from either the transcript(s) or the recording(s).

( )c. If classified PERMISSION REQUIRED, permission must be obtained in writing from the interviewee before the transcribed interview(s) can be examined or the tape recording(s) audited.

( )d. If classified CLOSED, the transcribed interview(s) and the tape recording(s) will be sealed until a time specified by the interviewee. This may be until the death of the interviewee or for any specified number of years.

2. It is expressly understood that in giving this authorization, I am in no way precluded from placing such restrictions as I may desire upon use of the interview at any time during my lifetime, nor does this authorization in any way affect my rights to the copyright of my literary expressions that may be contained in the interview.

Witness my hand and seal this 23rd day of October 1971.

E. J. Hedding

I hereby accept and consent to the foregoing Declaration of Trust and the powers therein conferred upon me as Trustee:

T. J. Hedding #1 - 1

Interview Number 1 with Vice Admiral Truman J. Hedding,
U.S. Navy (Retired)

Place: Admiral Hedding's home, Coronado, California

Date: Saturday, 27 February 1971

Interviewer: Etta-Belle Kitchen

Q: I appreciate being able to talk with you. Your career is distinguished and has had many highlights. I know that the Institute will benefit by having your recollections and appreciate your being able to do the interview.

I think we might begin with a thumbnail sketch of your early days, Admiral. If you would give me some of the vital statistics, we could begin with that.

Admiral Hedding: I was born on Bastille Day, the 14th day of July 1902 in Morrisdale, Pennsylvania. My father was a doctor, Dr. Benjamin Hedding, and my mother was from Delaware.

I grew up in Pennsylvania. I was about 10 or 11 years old when we moved out to New Mexico. Actually, we moved out there for my health. We lived in the little town of Mountainair, I guess 50 or 60 miles from Albuquerque, New Mexico. Mountainair was just a little, tiny place, and I imagine it still is. My father practiced there. As I said, the reason we came out there was for my health.

Schooling there was rather primitive, in that they

only had three months of school. Then we'd go into Albuquerque and try to get some more schooling. So I really didn't get any formal schooling until much later on when we moved to Santa Fe, New Mexico.

To backtrack a little bit--when I was still in school in Albuquerque and Santa Fe there was a teacher who intrigued me, and got me very interested in mathematics. I just kind of became a bug on it and just loved it.

At that time I became interested in the Naval Academy. My father, through local friends, arranged for me to take the competitive exam for the Naval Academy by our one congressman at large in New Mexico, the Honorable Benigno C. Hernandez. I took the competitive exam and came out second. Immediately after that I took the entrance exam to the Naval Academy, which I passed with very modest grades while I was still in East Denver High School. The principal got into the Naval Academy.* He had prepared back in Washington and was much better prepared than I. He won out and got the principal appointment, although he only lasted one year at the Naval Academy.

So, having passed the entrance exam, I had no problems getting an appointment for the class of 1924. I was supposed to report in June, but I had an appendectomy and didn't get in until September.

---

*Each congressmen was allotted some principal appointments and in addition arranged for a series of alternates to receive the appointment if the principal nominee failed to pass the physical or mental requirements for admission.

The year I was waiting to get into the Naval Academy, I took a year at Denver University. I just picked the things I liked. Mostly they were mathematics--calculus and integral equations and things that I was interested in--and a course in the slide rule. So by the time I got to the Naval Academy, and with so much of the course based on mathematics, it was relatively easy. And having grown up in New Mexico, I spoke Spanish reasonably well. So I was smart and chose Spanish as my language. So I had no problems academically, and graduated six in my class.*

Q: Are there any highlights from your four years at the academy?

Admiral Hedding: I think it was a very normal midshipman tour. I was on the soccer squad and the track team.

Of course, today the youngsters have so many things they can do. There are so many elective courses that they can take. We had no real electives at all. We only had one elective course; you took Spanish or French. Other than that, we all got the same thing. We were given more of a technical education to teach us to be naval officers, rather than a liberal arts course.

---

*The Naval Academy class of 1924 was made up of 522 graduates.

T. J. Hedding #1 - 4

Q: The degree you had is bachelor of science?

Admiral Hedding: That's what you get from the Naval Academy. You're given a bachelor of science degree. Of course, later on I got my master's at MIT, which I'll cover later.* So it was a very normal tour at the Naval Academy.

Upon graduation I reported to the battleship Maryland.** At that time they were sending all of the graduates to battleships or cruisers. The idea was that you really didn't start learning to be a naval officer until you actually reported aboard a ship, and, of course, the life aboard battleships was typical Navy at that time. You had a junior officers' mess and a wardroom mess.

The life at that time in the junior mess was a lot of fun. And we had a magnificent salary of $143.00 a month. So we'd pay our mess bills so we could eat. Then we'd go ashore and spend the rest. If we ran out of money, we'd stay aboard ship until next payday.

I reported aboard at Puget Sound. Most of the time we were in the San Pedro area. Then in '25 the fleet left for a cruise to Australia. First we spent some time in Hawaii,

---

*MIT--Massachusetts Institute of Technology.
**The USS Maryland (BB-46) was commissioned 21 July 1921. She had a standard displacement of 32,600 tons, was 624 feet long and 98 feet in the beam. Her top speed was 21.2 knots. She was armed with eight 16-inch guns and 12 5-inch broadside guns. She remained in active service until decommissioned on 3 April 1947, following World War II.

and that was a lot of fun. That was back in 1925, and Hawaii was quite different. At that time there was only one hotel, the Moana on Waikiki Beach. To get there you'd have to take an open-air trolley across the marsh where Kapiolani Park is now, on out to the Moana. They still have the big banyan tree in the court. Running out from the banyan tree, way out on the reef, was a bandstand on the reef. We'd go out there at night in the bandstand, with the great big moon, and the beach boys singing. It was really something. The bandstand was washed away in one of the Kona storms later on, and they never rebuilt it.

We went to Australia. That was a most interesting trip for me, because I was assistant navigator. A new navigator reported aboard, Commander Van Valkenburgh.* He was the commanding officer of the Arizona on 7 December 1941, was lost in the Arizona, and his body is still there.

He had been on engineering duty, and he said he was not very familiar with navigation. I would be the navigator, and he would be the assistant navigator. So that's the way we worked it from Samoa to Sydney. I brought the ship in and anchored it as navigator. We spent two weeks in Sydney, and we just really had a ball there. Australia just went all out; they did everything for us. We even had tickets for any trolley or any railroad train or anything. We went all over that part of Australia.

---

*Lieutenant Commander Franklin Van Valkenburgh, USN.

T. J. Hedding #1 - 6

Then we had five days at sea. Then we had two weeks at Auckland, New Zealand, and then we came home.

When we got home, back to San Pedro, I had become interested in naval aviation. Particularly at that time I thought I wanted to be an aircraft designer. We had three naval aviators on the Maryland. The senior aviator was Art Davis; another was W. W. Smith; and Apollo Soucek, whom you have heard about.* W. W. Smith and Apollo were assigned as assistants to the assistant navigator for the cruise to Australia. So I got to be very interested in aviation and talked to them about it. I said, "I want to design airplanes."

They said, "Where do you stand in your class?" And I told them. They said, "You can get in the Construction Corps easily if you want to, and then you can shift over to aircraft design. Then if you really want to be an aviator, you can maybe get down to Pensacola and get your wings."

I said, "What's the other out?"

"The other out is to go to Pensacola first and get your wings. And then some time subsequent to that, put in for a postgraduate course in aeronautical engineering."

I said, "That sounds good to me. I don't want to be just a Construction Corps type." So I put in for Pensacola. When we got back from Australia, I went aboard the hospital ship Mercy and took my flight physical, along

─────────────
*Lieutenant Arthur C. Davis, USN; Lieutenant (junior grade) Walton W. Smith, USN; Lieutenant Apollo Soucek, USN.

T. J. Hedding #1 - 7

with my roommate on the <u>Maryland</u>. I passed, but he didn't, so he didn't get to go at that time.

I was then ordered, in December of 1925, to report to Pensacola for temporary duty for instruction in aviation. I stayed there a year and got my wings, and was ordered to Fighting Squadron One, the old High Hat squadron. The commander of the squadron was Lieutenant Bogan.* That's where I first met Jerry. He was a bachelor, and he was something. The whole group of us were young and full of beans, and we just had a grand time. Everything we did was just fun.

Q: I gather that each step that you went along you liked.

Admiral Hedding: I loved everything that I did in the Navy.

Q: Did you like flying?

Admiral Hedding: I was crazy about it; I really was. I was always so glad I was always a fighter pilot. I've always looked upon the fighter pilots as being the cream of the crop in most ways. They selected ten of us out of the whole group of students to get fighter training. Now they

---
*Lieutenant Gerald F. Bogan, USN. Bogan eventually retired as a vice admiral. His oral history is in the Naval Institute collection.

T. J. Hedding #1 - 8

give all the same training. But we were a select group. From there we went directly to fighter squadrons. As I said, I came to VF-1.

Q: Do you think you have to like it to do it well?

Admiral Hedding: Certainly. Anything you do well, you have to like. And you have to be highly motivated to do things well. You must not shy away from difficult jobs. A lot of naval officers have failed to go as far as they should because they are always looking for easy jobs.

I was in Fighting Squadron One for two years. I made jaygee then, while I was in VF-1.* I was ordered to Annapolis, Maryland, for a postgraduate course in aeronautical engineering.

Q: Did you ask for it?

Admiral Hedding: Oh, yes. You had to put in for it, and you had to be selected. Three of us--Cato Glover, Swede Ekstrom, and I--were the first naval aviators to be ordered to take the course in structures and design, which previously only the naval constructors had taken.** We were ordered to the Postgraduate School in Annapolis,

---
*Jaygee--lieutenant (junior grade).
**Lieutenant Cato D. Glover, Jr., USN; Lieutenant (junior grade) Clarence E. Ekstrom, USN.

Maryland, for a refresher course and to get us back into a student regime.

MIT was tough, and when we got up there, we found out how tough it was. We were in competition in this aeronautical engineering course with kids that had just completed four years at MIT and were embarked upon their postgraduate courses to get their degrees. So they were in the business of studying, and it was difficult for us to get back into the habit of study.

Q: When you went to the Postgraduate School, did you know you were going on to MIT?

Admiral Hedding: Yes, that was part of it. You were sent to the Postgraduate School in Annapolis to refresh you. It was preparatory. Before the normal course up there, the three of us took summer school at MIT. Then we went on to those courses to get our degree, and write our thesis for our master's degree.

Q: Do you recall what your thesis was?

Admiral Hedding: Yes. It was theoretical, to determine from wind-tunnel tests the stability features of a real airplane. We had a lot of wind-tunnel data on a type of

T. J. Hedding #1 - 10

trainer that was out at the air station at Squantum.*
Swede Ekstrom and I collaborated on our thesis. We did the
flying, and by shifting the center of gravity and other
things, we could determine whether or not our mathematical
analysis of wind-tunnel data could be confirmed by our
actual testing of the airplane. So that was our thesis.

Q: Do you want to amplify on the courses that you took at
MIT?

Admiral Hedding: We were more or less the guinea pigs as
far as the Navy was concerned--to utilize naval aviators
rather than constructors and let us get an aeronautical
degree in structure and design. Maybe they had the idea in
the back of their heads that we would perhaps, being
aviators, be better designers of airplanes than those who
were not aviators and didn't really understand or have the
feel for flying that we did. I think that was probably why
we were selected. I don't know what they've done later on.
It's become very, very technical now.

Actually, I think the Navy, to a degree, wasted money
on us, because only at one time subsequent to my getting my
degree and going to MIT did I have any duty where I could
use the knowledge acquired up there. I did at one time
later on have the propeller desk in the Bureau of

---

*Naval air station, Squantum, Massachusetts, near Boston.

Aeronautics, so what I had done at MIT helped.

Upon getting my degree, I was assigned to the Flight Test Section, which was then at Anacostia. That was quite a feather. Everybody wanted to be a test pilot, and I thought it was great.

Q: Did it seem romantic at the time?

Admiral Hedding: Sure, flying is romantic; it always will be.

That was the first time I got to know Ralph Ofstie; he was in charge of the Flight Test Section at Anacostia.* There were three or four nice people there. There was Joe Bolger, who is, of course, retired.** There was Trapnell, whom you may have heard of, and Bob Pirie and I.*** That was the Flight Test Section. Later they moved the Flight Test Section from Anacostia down to Patuxent because of the dangers of testing planes.**** We had some planes crack up, so they thought it best to get it away from that populated area.

---

*Lieutenant Ralph A. Ofstie, USN. Ofstie was later a vice admiral and served as Commander Sixth Fleet.
**Lieutenant Joseph F. Bolger, USN. He retired in 1953 as a vice admiral.
***Lieutenant Frederick M. Trapnell, USN, who later ran Flight Test himself and eventually retired as a vice admiral. Lieutenant (junior grade) Robert B. Pirie, USN. Pirie eventually became a vice admiral and served as Deputy Chief of Naval Operations (Air).
****The naval air station at Patuxent River, Maryland, was established in November 1942 to facilitate the testing of experimental aircraft.

T. J. Hedding #1 - 12

Q: Did you have any close calls during your testing?

Admiral Hedding: You always do. A lot of times you get scared. Things happen and you get scared. Anybody that didn't get scared just doesn't know what he was talking about.

I went to the Flight Test Section, and while I was there I made lieutenant. From there I was ordered to the USS Saratoga.* I reported aboard, and I had many different duties. I was the hangar deck officer, the gasoline officer, the assembly and repair officer. Then they moved me up to the flight deck, and I had the flight deck for a while. Then the landing signal officer was suddenly detached.

The then executive officer, Commander Kelly Turner, called me in and said, "Truman, you are now going to be the landing signal officer.** You're going to bring the planes aboard--flag waving." With Dutch Duerfeldt, who was then the landing signal officer, I spent about two weeks in the San Diego area learning to be a landing signal

---
*The USS Saratoga (CV-3) was commissioned 16 November 1927 She had a standard displacement of 33,000 tons, was 888 feet long, 106 feet beam, and had a draft of 24 feet. She had a top speed of 33.9 knots. Following her World War II service she was sunk in atomic bomb tests in July 1946.
**Commander Richmond Kelly Turner, USN, later a four-star admiral and top amphibious commander in World War II.

officer.*

Q: I would think that would be a terribly difficult and almost frightening and responsible position.

Admiral Hedding: It was, in a way, but having been a naval officer and having been a carrier pilot, it was a very normal thing. I knew pretty much what it was all about. I did need some training.

I went to see Commander Turner and said, "Let's don't ever have this thing happen again, where suddenly you detach the landing signal officer and you bring somebody new in here and it may not work out. I think I should have a couple of assistants."

He said, "I think so too. Who do you want?"

So I picked out a couple of classmates, Al Handly and Bill Davis, the one who flew with Goebel on the first flight to Hawaii as navigator.** Also Bill was a member of the first Navy stunt team. He and Putt Storrs and Tomlinson were the original three Sea Hawks.***

---
*Lieutenant (junior grade) Clifford H. Duerfeldt, USN.
**Lieutenant Albert Handly, USN; Lieutenant William V. Davis, Jr., USN. In August 1927 Arthur Goebel flew from Oakland, California, to Hawaii with Lieutenant Davis as navigator. Their plane finished first among 16 entrants in a contest for $35,000 in prizes offered by James B. Dole for a nonstop flight to Hawaii. Only Goebel's plane and one other made the complete flight successfully.
***This group was the forerunner of today's Blue Angels. The other members were Lieutenant (junior grade) Aaron P. Storrs III, USN, and Lieutenant Daniel W. Tomlinson, USN. The oral history of Tomlinson is in the USNI collection.

T. J. Hedding #1 - 14

I was the landing signal officer, and that was most interesting, but I wanted to get in a squadron. So I asked to be ordered from the <u>Saratoga</u> to a <u>Saratoga</u> squadron, and I was. Normally when ordered to a squadron you qualify by landing. I had always made it a point to land the type of plane that every squadron ever had aboard myself, to make me a better landing signal officer.

I was ordered to report to Fighting Squadron Six, with none other than my old friend Ralph Ofstie as the squadron commander. I spent a year in Fighting Squadron Six. The <u>Saratoga</u> was operating in the Pacific off of Pearl Harbor. During that time, reminiscing a bit, in one of our operations we attacked Pearl Harbor in almost the identical way the Japs did on the seventh of December of 1941.* We came in from the north and made our attacks. I don't know whether they read our reports on it, but they did practically the same thing in 1941.

Q: Do you know if your game was the first one of that type to use that strategy?

Admiral Hedding: I'm not sure whether it was or not, but I knew we did that, and we did the same thing again.

---

*This exercise took place on 7 February 1932. For another account, see Admiral Arthur W. Radford, "Aircraft Battle Force," in <u>Air Raid: Pearl Harbor!</u> (Annapolis: Naval Institute Press, 1981), pages 18-22.

Again reminiscing, at that time we had a remarkable officer in command of the Air Force Battle Fleet, Admiral Joseph Reeves, known as Billy Goat Reeves.* He was a very brilliant man. He was not a professional naval aviator. He was one of those who came in aviation late and got observer's wings. He was a very keen strategist and tactician. He made us do a lot of things off the Langley, the Saratoga, and the Lexington that we really didn't know if we could do or not. This was while I was on the Saratoga in the fighter squadron.

I remember while I was on the Saratoga, in VF-6, also that year we made an attack on the Panama Canal. Admiral Reeves detached the Saratoga, and we went way down past the Galapagos Islands and came in and made an attack on the Panama Canal. That was quite a business. We flew over water about 150 miles and then back to the carrier, and we didn't have all the aids that they have today. That was a long flight.

We were doing things then that we really didn't know we could do. Naval aviation at that time was a small group. We were learning an awful lot. We were just getting real carriers. The Langley, as you know, was a converted collier, and we learned in that. Then we got the Saratoga and the Lexington, originally designed to be

---

*Rear Admiral Joseph M. Reeves, USN, Commander Carrier Divisions U.S. Fleet. His nickname stemmed from his goatee beard.

battle cruisers and were made into carriers.

Then from there on we started to grow. We started to do things and to learn things--like that attack on Honolulu when I was in VF-6. We had no running lights on the planes; we had no radio. We decided that we would make a dawn attack on Pearl Harbor, so we took off. We all had flashlights, and we would flash these flashlights over our right shoulder so we could better rendezvous in the dark. But we never did, and we didn't rendezvous until practically over Diamond Head at dawn. Anyway, we all got together for the attack on Pearl Harbor, and we all got back safely. We were doing things.

Admiral Reeves has never been given the credit that he should have been given in the development of naval aviation. He was a great man. I first was with him when he was Captain Reeves on the old North Dakota, on one of my midshipman's cruises.* He was quite a student of naval strategy. He used to lecture on the Battle of Jutland. I just don't think he has been given the credit by naval historians for getting us in our formative years. He was making us do things, so we were learning to do things with carriers that we didn't think we could do. I think someone should really write something about Admiral Reeves, because he was a great man.

Then I reported to the Bureau of Aeronautics for duty.
_____
*Reeves commanded the battleship North Dakota (BB-29) in 1922-23.

T. J. Hedding #1 - 17

At that particular time the Chief of the Bureau of Aeronautics was quite a character himself, Ernest J. King.* We all called him "Uncle Ernie." Uncle Ernie worked hard, and he played hard. He really did; he played hard. He would go to cocktail parties in Washington. He and Mrs. King would arrive, and they would spend about an hour or so, a respectable time. Then he'd take Mrs. King home and he'd come back.

Admiral King was really quite something. I knew him when he commanded the Lexington, and, of course, I got to know him quite well in the Bureau of Aeronautics.** He got somewhat in disfavor later on in his career, and he was ordered to the Navy General Board, which at that time was kind of a receiving barracks for the senior admirals. Just prior to their retirement, they were ordered to the General Board. Supposedly they were to advise the Secretary of the Navy on various subjects, using their tremendous background and experience. Admiral King wanted none of it.***

I always admired him, and I always talked back to him. As a matter of fact, when he was Commander Air Force Pacific I was just about to be ordered to command Fighting Squadron Two.**** I would be the first man in my class to

---
*Rear Admiral Ernest J. King, USN, who later became a fleet admiral and served as Chief of Naval Operations and Commander in Chief U.S. Fleet during World War II.
**Captain King commanded the Lexington (CV-2), 1930-32, during part of the time Hedding was in her sister Saratoga.
***Rear Admiral King served on the General Board 1939-40.
****As a vice admiral, King served as Commander Aircraft Battle Force in 1938-39.

T. J. Hedding #1 - 18

get command of a squadron. At that time I was called up to the office. Captain Kelly Turner was the chief of staff.* I said, "What does the admiral want to see me about, Captain?"

He said, "Well, Truman, he wants you to be his flag lieutenant."

I said, "He does?"

He said, "Yes."

I said, "Well, gee, can I be frank?"

He said, "Sure."

I said, "I don't want the job. I know it's an honor, but I'm just about to get command of this squadron, and that's the greatest thing that could happen to me."

He said, "Well, go in and tell the admiral how you feel."

So I went in, and he said, "Did Captain Turner tell you why I asked to see you?"

And I said, "Yes, sir, he did."

He said, "What do you think of it?"

I said, "Admiral, that would be quite an honor, but can I be frank?"

He said, "Sure."

I said, "I've just gotten a letter from Washington that I'm about to be ordered to command Fighting Squadron

---

*Actually in late 1939 Captain Richmond K. Turner, USN, was commanding officer of the cruiser Astoria (CA-34). Captain John H. Hoover, USN, was chief of staff, AirBatFor.

T. J. Hedding #1 - 19

Two. I think that would be the greatest thing that ever happened to me."

He said, "Well, I guess it would be okay." So I got out of that job with Admiral Ernest J. King.

So again I knew him in Washington. I went to call on him when he was on the Navy General Board. I said, "Admiral, what in the world are you doing here?"

He said, "Well, I don't like it a bit. One of these days they're going to need a son of a bitch, and they're going to ask for me."

From there he was ordered to command something in the Atlantic Fleet.* Then when the war came along, President Roosevelt brought him in to take over the Navy during World War II as CominCh.** He was really something.

Q: In your duties on the propeller desk did you use the knowledge you had gained?

Admiral Hedding: Yes, and that's about the only time I ever used it. Actually, I think it's wrong to take professional naval aviators, the people that like to fly, and make them technicians. I think they should be technicians, period, like they do now. I think that's one

---
*In December 1940, as a vice admiral, King became Commander Patrol Force in the Atlantic. In February 1941 the billet was upgraded to four stars and became Commander in Chief Atlantic Fleet.
**From 1941 to 1945 Admiral King served as Commander in Chief U.S. Fleet, abbreviated CominCh.

of the reasons why they set up the aeronautical engineering duty only branch of the Navy. They never commanded anything; they never commanded squadrons. They could go to sea in more or less of a technical position on somebody's staff, but I didn't want that.

When I went to the bureau they asked me if I wanted to go AEDO, and I said, "No, I don't want any part of it."

Q: You also had some additional duties while you were in BuAer.

Admiral Hedding: Yes. I was then a bachelor. Lieutenant Commander J. E. Ostrander was the senior naval aide at the White House.* Ozzie, as we knew him out here on the West Coast, was a naval aviator. He was on duty in Washington, and he asked me would I like to be an aide at the White House. I said, "Well, I don't know. What is it?"

He explained it and said, "You'll have a lot of fun."

Q: I understood there were three requirements--that you were single, tall, and good looking.

Admiral Hedding: I don't know about that. I was tall and single. I enjoyed it; it really was fun. There were a lot of interesting things you got to do and see, and a lot of

---
*Lieutenant Commander John E. Ostrander, Jr., USN.

T. J. Hedding #1 - 21

people you never would see otherwise.

Q: Can you give me a picture of the White House in those days?

Admiral Hedding: The White House in those days was quite social. The President enjoyed these parties, I think, much more than Mrs. Roosevelt did. We had the normal congressional receptions for the armed forces and for the diplomatic corps.

The White House aides were just more or less glorified ushers. We handled the people when they came in. The protocol was quite elaborate, and things had to be handled very carefully, or feelings would be hurt among the foreign service people there. At that time Captain Wilson Brown was the naval aide to the President.* General Pa Watson was the Army aide.**

These receptions were quite elaborate. You'd come there to, say, a diplomatic reception where there would be a whole bunch of ambassadors and ministers and their wives. They all had to be presented to the President and Mrs. Roosevelt in order of their seniority. The seniority was determined by the date they presented their credentials to

---

*Captain Wilson Brown, USN, served in that capacity from June 1934 to May 1936.
**Colonel Edwin M. Watson, USA, was President Roosevelt's military aide. He held the post from 1933 until his death in early 1945, when he was a major general.

the President. There might be some little country that would have the senior diplomat.

We had a room down in the basement. We'd get our orders of the day, and each one of us would be given a little card. The group coming in would be divided into about four groups. On your card would be the name of the people. When they were announced by an aide at the entrance to the East Room, you would take them to your part of the East Room and keep them together. You'd say, "Now, you stand there. Don't go moving around." Because you had to bring them to be presented in the right order. On your card would be the Ambassador and Madam So-and-so of whatever country it was. And then opposite that would be his dinner partner, whom he would escort into the dining room.

He was given a card when he came in with the name of his dinner partner. Then you'd ask him--did he know So-and-so? If he didn't, then while you were doing all of this, you would grab him and take him over and introduce him to his dinner partner. When it was all over, the President and Mrs. Roosevelt would start the grand entrance to the dining room. Everybody would be lined up, and they would get their partners, and away they'd go.

Q: That was quite a logistic problem, wasn't it?

Admiral Hedding: It was fun.

Then we would go down into the room that we had. They would have sandwiches and coffee down there for us while they were all eating. Then after their dinner was through, they'd usually come into the East Room and have some kind of entertainment, not as elaborate as brought in by the Kennedys. Then it would be over about 11:00 o'clock.

You'd never know when you'd be called by one of the secretaries of Mrs. Roosevelt that she'd be having a tea, and they'd need a couple of aides to stand in line and introduce people. So we always had to keep a uniform ready if they called, and run and go to the White House.

Q: You never did in the day?

Admiral Hedding: In the daytime, too, for receptions and teas.

Q: It surprised me that you'd be taken away from your job to do that.

Admiral Hedding: Oh, yes.

Mrs. Roosevelt was a very lovely person. She did an awfully nice thing for me, which I'll never forget. Any time one of the aides' mothers would come to Washington,

Mrs. Roosevelt would always ask her to attend one of her teas. You would go down there with your mother--not as an aide, just go to a tea.

My mother came to Washington, and we were invited to go to a tea. Just about that time Colonel Howe died.* So her secretary called me up and said, "Lieutenant, I'm sorry. You know that Colonel Howe died. The Roosevelts have canceled all their social schedule, everything."

So I said to Mother, "It's too bad that you didn't get to the White House."

A couple of days went by, and I got another call from the secretary. She said, "Mrs. Roosevelt asks that you and your mother come to tea, if you can, tomorrow afternoon at 5:00 o'clock." It was to be in the Red Room or the Green Room, one of the small sitting rooms there. We went there, just Mother and me and an Episcopal minister. Mrs. Roosevelt had done that just for me. She'd found out that my mother was there and the reception was called off.

So those are some of the highlights.

Q: Did you have any personal contact with the President?

Admiral Hedding: Very little. He was a most unusual person. At these big receptions they would always line up in the East Room and would come through the Red Room into

---
*Louis A. Howe was a long-time confidant and adviser to Franklin D. Roosevelt. He died 18 April 1936.

the Blue Room, which is the big oval room. He had a specially built chair that he would sit on. He would take 200 at a time. Gus Gingrich, who was the bodyguard, had a clicker. Standing right in front of the President were what we called the Four Horsemen: Navy, Army, Navy, Army. We would stand there all braced up. This was the atmosphere as the people went by. Gus Gingrich would always make some crack about, "Look at this babe coming."

Then at 200 he'd say, "Two hundred, Mr. President. Stop the line." We'd stop the line, he'd relax and have a cigarette, and then say, "Let's go some more."

Q: You are tall and strong, and I have heard on occasion he would have a naval aide by him so he could stand.

Admiral Hedding: Yes, he would. It was usually that or one of his sons. James was about my age, I guess, and John and FDR, Jr. They would help him. Of course, Gus Gingrich would do it all the time. The President, you know, was completely paralyzed from the waist down. To sit down he would stand up. Then he would say, "Okay," and he'd break the braces, and down he'd go. Then when he'd get up, he'd hit them, make a whack, and then he'd get up and he could walk.

Then I reported to Fighting Squadron Two, the enlisted

men's squadron. I first reported as executive officer. Then I fleeted up about a year later as commanding officer. In the meantime, I made lieutenant commander. The enlisted pilots in the Navy seldom became more than second pilots in a big boat squadron or in the utility squadrons. So somebody got the idea, "Let's get the cream of the crop and set up a fighter squadron and order these enlisted pilots as the wingmen." All the section leaders were officers. There were seven of us, including the liaison plane. Our wingmen were all enlisted pilots. One who flew in my section, Sam Lofton, is now one of the councilmen over in San Diego.

Q: How did they get to be pilots?

Admiral Hedding: Just like we did, went to Pensacola. They had gone through the school.

So I enjoyed it very much. They were all hotshot pilots, excellent pilots. They certainly kept the officers on their toes. To be able to lead them was something.

While I was there I made lieutenant commander.

Q: Did you enjoy that?

Admiral Hedding: Very much. That's when we were getting along to just before the war.

Q: This was the first time you'd been a commanding officer.

Admiral Hedding: Yes, and you worked a long time to get it. Of course, now the squadron commanders are much more senior than we were then, because there are a lot more squadrons.

In 1940 we went to Hawaii on our fleet problem. While we were there, all transfers were frozen, because there was a war alert. I had an awful time getting relieved so I could report to Pensacola for duty. I finally got orders to go, and I had to go up to the commander in chief to get authority to go back on a destroyer because they just weren't letting anybody go.

Q: Why did you want to go back to Pensacola?

Admiral Hedding: Why stay on? The officer to relieve me in command was aboard ready to take over the squadron. I already had orders to Pensacola. I wanted to go to Pensacola. It was a tour that I hadn't had, and I thought it would be fun and I'd enjoy it.

To get back to the West Coast I had to be ordered to a destroyer. They were sending some destroyers back; that was in May 1940. I got orders to report aboard the USS

Macdonough. The commanding officer was Commander Ray Tarbuck.* So I got back and went to Pensacola. They put me in charge of Corry and Saufley fields. Of course, I was there when Pearl Harbor hit. As of matter of fact, I had the command duty the day that Pearl Harbor was attacked.

I was in my quarters, and my mother was listening to the national symphony. They broke in and said, "There's been an attack on Pearl Harbor." I headed back because we had some VIPs aboard: Artemus Gates, the assistant secretary of the Navy for Air was down, with a couple of his assistants: O. B. Hardison; Art Radford; the skipper of the station, Putty Read of NC-4 fame; Bill Sample; and Windy Switzer.** They were all out playing golf. So I sent the duty officer out to get them, got their crew together, and sent them to Washington.

Q: What was your reaction? Do you remember?

Admiral Hedding: I just couldn't believe it. We had so many rumors of what the damage was, we didn't know; they weren't putting any information out. All these battleships

---
*Lieutenant Commander Ray D. Tarbuck, USN. Tarbuck's oral history is in the Naval Institute collection.
**Captain Osborne B. Hardison, USN, was Gates's aide; Commander Arthur W. Radford, USN, was director of aviation training in the Bureau of Aeronautics; Captain Albert C. Read, USN, who had been in command of the NC-4 mission across the Atlantic in 1919, was in 1941 in command of the naval air station at Pensacola; Commander William D. Sample was Read's executive officer; Commander Wendell G. Switzer, USN, was also on Read's staff.

were sunk and the carriers were sunk.* We didn't know. Everybody was taking crazy precautions--trying to spread the planes out on the training field so that the Japanese wouldn't destroy our training planes, silly things like that. Or putting a watch over the water main from Pensacola to the air station. Of course, we didn't go nearly as crazy as they did out on the West Coast or in Hawaii.

The Japanese, even when things were going really well with them, never did intend to invade Hawaii. We didn't know it then. When I interrogated them later, on the bombing survey, I asked, "Did you ever have any ideas about invading Hawaii?"

They said, "No, we wanted to sink the fleet. We thought if we sank the fleet and made the war difficult enough, the American people would say, 'Let's get out of it,' and we would achieve our aims in Southeast Asia."

They meant to attack Pearl Harbor and might have come back again, but they had no intention of effecting a landing there.

Q: Their purpose was to do just they did do.

Admiral Hedding: That's right.

---

*In fact, no carriers were sunk during the Japanese attack.

T. J. Hedding #1 - 30

Q: Did they express disappointment at not having found the aircraft carriers there?

Admiral Hedding: They thought they'd sunk one aircraft carrier. We had the old Utah as a target. It had an armored deck, and we would bomb it. We had remote control from another ship, and that was one of our targets that we used to bomb here off San Diego. They sank that, and I think reported one carrier sunk. But the rest of the carriers were out, fortunately. We got smart on that.

Q: Do you have any ideas on that?

Admiral Hedding: I think it's probably in the book. I haven't gotten to the point yet where I've dug into that-- why Halsey and the carriers were out at that particular time.*

Actually, Halsey was on his way back to Pearl. A classmate of mine, Brom Nichol, was on his staff, and he was to come in early to carry some message from Halsey to Admiral Kimmel.** He was in the back seat of this scouting plane, and they were flying over Ewa when the

---
*Vice Admiral William F. Halsey, USN, was at sea in command of Task Force Eight, built around the carrier Enterprise (CV-6), which had delivered a Marine Fighter Squadron 221 to Wake Island on 4 December.
**Admiral Husband E. Kimmel, USN, was Commander in Chief Pacific Fleet. Lieutenant Commander Bromfield B. Nichol, USN.

Japanese attacked, and their plane was shot at by the Japanese. They finally struggled in over Ewa plantation and landed on Ford Island, just as the whole thing was going up in flames. They couldn't believe it. At first they thought these crazy Air Corps boys from Wheeler Field were coming down and diving at them.* Then they saw the red ball on the side of the plane, and it became a different game. Then they could see all the flames and smoke and everything else.

When Pearl Harbor came along, we immediately started to expand Pensacola as fast as we could. We'd already started before that, but that really built a fire under it. Captain Read put me in charge of the expansion of all the new fields in Pensacola--to select the sites and all that business. So that's what I was doing, but I said, "This is no place to be with a war going on." So I asked to be sent to sea in a carrier. You always have friends somewhere that you can ask for things. I've always been a firm believer in asking for what I want, and then working like hell to get it. Friends always help you out. If you want something bad enough, why shouldn't you try to get it? So that's what I would do.

I got orders to report in 1942 to the Newport News Shipbuilding and Dry Dock Company, in connection with the

---
*The official name was U.S. Army Air Forces from 1941 to 1947, when the U.S. Air Force was established. However, throughout the oral history Admiral Hedding refers to it as the Air Corps. That was the official name up to 1941 and remained in common use for many years afterward.

fitting out of the USS Essex, the first of our new carriers.* It was one of the hardest jobs I ever had, I think, in my whole career.

Admiral King had promised the President that the first of the new carriers would be commissioned in 1942--or else. So we were commissioned on New Year's Eve 1942, and the ship was not completely ready. It was towed down to the Navy yard at Portsmouth, and the ship was completed there.** Being the first of a class, it's always difficult when there are so many things to be done with a new type.

I reported first as air officer. There were two members of the class of '22, and two in the class of '23, who, of course, were senior to me. I was the only one selected on the first go-around as commander. Then my orders were changed to order me as executive officer, putting me above these other people, which was a rather trying experience, but it worked out all right.

A couple of them didn't turn out too well. I knew who the prospective commanding officer was going to be, Captain Donald Duncan.*** He was then on Admiral King's staff in

---

*The USS Essex (CV-9) was the first of the large new carriers. She had a standard displacement of 27,100 tons, compared with 19,800 tons for the preceding Yorktown (CV-5) class. The Essex was 872 feet long and had an extreme width of 148 feet on the flight deck. She had a top speed of 33 knots and could carry more than 80 aircraft.
**Norfolk Navy Yard, Portsmouth, Virginia.
***Captain Donald B. Duncan, USN, who eventually became a four-star admiral and Vice Chief of Naval Operations. His oral history is in the Columbia University collection.

T. J. Hedding #1 - 33

Washington, so I'd fly up there and give progress reports. I told him we had a couple of officers I didn't think measured up. He said, "Who are they?" and I told him. They were detached, and we got two more. You have to do things like that in wartime. You have to be somewhat hard, because the chips are down and you can't afford to have someone who is doubtful.

Q: I'd like to have you amplify the experience before the commissioning. I'm sure you went through much travail.

Admiral Hedding: One of the things you have to write up is the ship's organization bill and the watch, quarter, and station bill. A big carrier is a big city, and it has to be organized properly. Everybody has to know what he does, what he has to do when, when this happens and that happens. The only ship's organization bills that were available were from the carriers in peacetime. So I wrote to three of my friends who had been out there in Air Pacific as executive officers of the Yorktown, the Enterprise, and the Hornet to give me the dope. I got back, "We don't pay attention to it anyway. We're too busy. Do the best you can." So I sat down with the other officers, and we wrote up those bills. They turned out to be pretty good.

Being the first of a class, there are a lot of things that have to be done and are difficult to get done.

T. J. Hedding #1 - 34

Fortunately, the prospective commanding officer was in a position of power in Washington, so I could go up and tell him things, and he could get things done. For instance, they had a little, tiny emergency cabin up on the navigation bridge for the captain. There were no toilet facilities there at all, and the bunk was terrible.

I tried to get to the superintendent of shipbuilding. I said, "Look, you've got to put a shower and head up there, because the captain in wartime doesn't leave the bridge. When he has to go, he can't go running down to the cabin. Everything has to be there, because he'll live there. He'll never leave the bridge."

It was most difficult, and I went to see Captain Duncan and told him. He said, "Okay."

Pretty soon they called me and said, "How do you want it?"

Q: I was going to ask if you had anything to do with the actual construction.

Admiral Hedding: No, just things like that or recommending we have more 40-millimeter mounts and things like that. Of course, at that time we had these 5-inch turrets, which worked out pretty good. There never was a need for arresting gear forward--in other words to land over the bow--although I'd done that. I was the first to land on

T. J. Hedding #1 - 35

the <u>Lexington</u> over the bow. That was out on one of our trips in the Molokai Channel off of Hawaii. I was up with part of the squadron, the weather got bad, and they wanted to bring us back aboard. VF-2 was always up at the forward end of the flight deck. They didn't know what to do with all the planes, so they said, "How about landing over the bow?"

"Sure," so we came in and landed over the bow. They never did it again; it just wasn't a good thing to do.

We tried to train our air group, and train our ship's personnel, how to anchor the ship and how to do this and do that up in the Chesapeake Bay. You didn't have much water up there; it's rather shallow. So with a big ship when you try to head into the wind to land, we'd run out of sea room right off the reel. There was a bunch of LSTs training up there.* The LST skippers were probably brokerage clerks, etc., but they did a marvelous job.

Captain Duncan, up in Washington, got the idea of going down into the Gulf of Paria, down near Venezuela, for training. It's a big, open gulf, but there's two entrances. Both entrances to the Gulf of Paria were closed by minefields. So we came charging down, and it was an ideal place for training. We were the first carrier down there; we could fly all day long and didn't have to worry about submarines or anything. It was great.

---
*LSTs--tank landing ships, which were large seagoing landing craft that had largely Naval Reserve crews.

Then we came back and did our final fitting out. Then we headed for the Panama Canal, went through, and on to Pearl Harbor. We had just gotten there when I made captain, and I was relieved as executive officer of the Essex. I reported to Commander Carrier Division 11, who at that time was a brand-new rear admiral by the name of Radford. I had just reported in to him on his flagship, the Independence, when I got a change of orders. I was told later that Admiral Towers changed them.* They had me report to Admiral Pownall, who then was the senior carrier admiral in Air Pacific.** Our first operation, as I remember, was a raid on Marcus Island.

Q: Before you go on to that, would you tell me of the organization at that time? Was it then a fast carrier task force?

Admiral Hedding: No, at that time we had very few carriers. Actually, when the Essex reported out there, I think the Saratoga had been hit again or torpedoed. Of course, the Yorktown had been lost, and the Wasp had been lost. The old Big E, the Enterprise, was still in there. The Lexington had been lost. So there weren't too many carriers.

---
*Vice Admiral John H. Towers, USN, Commander Air Force Pacific Fleet.
**Rear Admiral Charles A. Pownall, USN, Commander Carrier Division Three. He was Commander Task Force 15 for the attack on Marcus Island.

While we were there and getting ready, things were building up, and Admiral Nimitz realized that we would probably have to revise the tactical instructions for carriers. So he created a board with Admiral Pownall as the senior member of it. However, he very seldom ever showed up, so I more or less ran the board. We set up a lot of models in our headquarters basement there. I remember some of the people there--a classmate of mine by the name of Beakley and a battleship admiral by the name of Bill Fechteler.*

We started learning to do things with carriers as we got more of them. We knew a lot about flying, and we'd learned a lot about tactics, but we had to learn to handle more carriers. We realized that never again would the carriers operate in support of the battle line. The fleet would be organized around the carriers, and the battleships and cruisers would be primarily for the carriers' protection.

So we developed a circular formation. It was just kicked around. Then we used it later on and found it to be very effective, with one or two carriers in the center and then another concentric ring of alternating battleships and cruisers that provided tremendous antiaircraft fire. Then

---

*Commander Wallace M. Beakley, USN, was later a vice admiral and Commander Seventh Fleet. Rear Admiral William M. Fechteler, USN, later became a four-star admiral and Chief of Naval Operations from 1951 to 1953.

outside of that would be a circular screen of destroyers, usually a squadron of destroyers if you could get that many. They provided not only antiaircraft protection, but they provided primarily the submarine protection. So we developed the concept there in the basement, and it worked out pretty well.

Then we came to not only handling just one task group built around two or three carriers; then we had two, three, and four task groups. That became quite a potent organization and became the fast carrier force. We had to draw up the necessary tactical instructions so the carrier task groups wouldn't be running into each other while operating. The basic thing that determined the formation was where the wind was, because the carriers have to turn into the wind to launch.

During that time we also developed the tactic of launching and recovering the fighter patrols and the ASW patrols by a carrier positioning itself with the task group, and being able to turn into the wind and get its planes off and on before it got too far outside of the protective screen.*

There were two methods--we called them Able and Baker--at that time.** We launched the aircraft by getting the carriers either to do it separately, or we'd have to turn the whole formation into the wind. When we

---
*ASW--antisubmarine warfare.
**Able and Baker were the words used for the letters A and B in the phonetic alphabet of the period.

made carrier strikes, we'd turn the whole task group into the wind. We continued to develop and refine the tactics as we got more and more carriers, battleships, cruisers, and destroyers. The fast carrier task force became bigger and bigger with more task groups. It was quite a job tactically to handle the many task groups.

Then we learned something else that I don't think has ever been written up, and which should be. That is that we always had troubles fueling. There were elaborate instructions on fueling. You had to have the wind just so much on one bow or the other, and you rigged all kinds of spring lines and breast lines to position the ships alongside each other. The poor tanker always had to make the approach on the big ships. It was a silly thing.

I remember we were off Tarawa one time, and I said to Admiral Pownall, "Look, isn't this the silliest thing you ever saw?" Here came a tanker, with a cruiser alongside, making an approach on a carrier. "We all know how to fly formation. Let's set the tanker up there and let everybody come up and make an approach on the tanker and just run the fuel lines across."

He said, "Maybe that will work. Let's try it." We tried it and we found that we didn't have to have the wind just right. We could even fuel down wind unless the seas got very bad. All we would do was run messenger lines across, a distance line, and fuel lines. It was very simple. You just flew formation, and it worked fine. If we hadn't done that, I don't know what would have happened.

One of our big problems operating in the Pacific was that the wind was practically always on our stern, from the northeast. We were always to go west. So every time we'd get going, we'd have to turn around and go east to get the planes aboard or take them off. We learned a lot of tactics, not just the tactics of handling task groups and the task force. It was a very interesting business.

Of course, one of the really good things about it was that we developed real ship handlers. I guess we're all ship handlers; if you scratch any naval officer under the skin, he's a boat steerer, whether he's an aviator or not. And we got people like Arleigh Burke to help further revise and refine these tactical instructions.* We had critiques after every operation. Everybody would get up and say what we did wrong, and what we should do to correct our mistakes.

Q: You were in the initial planning?

Admiral Hedding: Yes, when we first started building the fast carrier task force.

---

*Captain Arleigh Burke, USN, became chief of staff to Vice Admiral Marc A. Mitscher, USN, who was commander of the fast carrier task force in 1944 and 1945. Later, as an admiral, Burke was Chief of Naval Operations, 1955-61.

T. J. Hedding #1 - 41

Q: What was Rear Admiral Pownall's title?

Admiral Hedding: I'm sure when I reported to Admiral Pownall I reported to him as Commander Carrier Division Three. It was an administrative organization. It didn't have any bearing on what would be a task group. He was the senior carrier admiral.

His first operation was a raid on Marcus and Wake. We had another task group commanded by Admiral Montgomery. Then in our operations in the Gilberts, we had two or three task groups by that time. We had Montgomery and Ted Sherman.*

Q: I just wondered how large a force Admiral Pownall had when you first went out there.

Admiral Hedding: It varied. The administrative organization was meaningless, because the administrative title was Commander Carrier Division Three and assigned by Commander Air Force Pacific. There would be one or two or three carriers in that. What would be in a task group would depend upon how many ships Admiral Nimitz, as commander in chief, would make available and assign to

---

*For the Gilberts operation in November 1943, Pownall commanded Task Force 50 and Task Group 50.1; Rear Admiral A. W. Radford, USN, had Task Group 50.2; Rear Admiral A. E. Montgomery, USN, had Task Group 50.3; and Rear Admiral Frederick C. Sherman, USN, had Task Group 50.4.

T. J. Hedding #1 - 42

us.*

Q: But Admiral Pownall was in charge of all the carriers that were there at that time--is that correct?

Admiral Hedding: He was the senior carrier commander. Then when we'd embark on these operations he would be the officer in tactical command, even though Admiral Spruance would be in the New Jersey, his flagship, in one of the task groups.**

Q: Admiral Spruance wasn't there yet when you first went out?

Admiral Hedding: No.

Q: I was trying to get a picture of what it looked like to you in late 1943.

Admiral Hedding: We were just struggling to get enough ships together. We were making small raids, like those on Marcus and Wake.*** Our first real operation was the Gilberts.

---
*Admiral Chester W. Nimitz, USN, Commander in Chief Pacific Fleet from 1941 to 1945.
**Vice Admiral Raymond A. Spruance, USN, Commander Fifth Fleet.
***The strike against Marcus was on 1 September 1943 and the ones against Wake on 5 and 6 October.

T. J. Hedding #1 - 43

Q: In what ship did Admiral Pownall fly his flag?

Admiral Hedding: I'm trying to remember. We moved the staff around for each operation, and we probably had a different flagship. In that particular operation it was the new Yorktown, "The Fighting Lady," with that grand character Jocko Clark as the skipper.* Then we had the Hornet as flagship, the Bunker Hill, and the new Lexington. We would just select one ship as our flagship and move aboard, varying from operation to operation.

So, as I said, our first real operation was the Gilberts, from which we learned a lot. It was at the Gilberts that Admiral Radford had a task group.

Q: I'd like to have you give me as much detail as you can on the preparation for this, and what actually took place.

Admiral Hedding: The way it worked for an operation like this was that a decision would be made by the Joint Chiefs in Washington that we would do certain things in the Pacific. What would happen really was that Admiral Nimitz, as area commander, and his planners would say, "We should go into the Gilberts." So he would write up a plan and

---
*Captain Joseph J. Clark, USN, was the first commanding officer of the USS Yorktown (CV-10). Film footage of the ship's operations was made into a documentary movie titled The Fighting Lady.

send it back to CominCh for approval. If necessary, it would be discussed with the Joint Chiefs. Then Admiral Nimitz would be given authority to carry out this operation, this objective, this time. That, in turn, would determine how many ships you'd have--how many carriers and how many battleships and cruisers, etc.

Then he would draw up a plan. In general, he would state the objective of the plan, what he would like to have accomplished, and give certain timing, and a broad idea of what the operation would consist of. But he would never say how to do something. He would tell you what he wanted to be done, to the fleet commanders or the operational commander at sea, and he would tell you what forces you would have to do the job.

Then you would take that and sit down and broaden your plan, based on that. So then the task force would have a plan. First there would be Admiral Nimitz's plan. That would go to the fleet commander, who usually at that time was Spruance, and later on it was Admiral Halsey.

The planning would be coordinated with the Marines, the Army, and the amphibious command. All that had to be done under Commander Fifth Fleet, who would draw up his plan. Of course, he would have an annex in there of what the carrier task force should do, and what the amphibious should do, etc. Then we each, in turn, would write up our own operation orders. At that time in our operations orders we would designate the task group commanders and what ships they would have. We would outline the basic plan--what would be done and the timing.

The task group commanders would then take the task force operation orders and draw up their own operations orders, in which they would get into the details of the actual missions to be flown from what carrier--how many planes, how many fighters, how many dive-bombers, how many torpedo bombers, and what their particular targets would be. Then you were getting down to the meat of the thing. Once we would issue our order, we would more or less ride along, just like Admiral Spruance was riding along, or Admiral Lee, who had the battleships.* They'd just ride along.

Each carrier task group, of course, had an officer in tactical command, an aviation admiral. He would command that task group, even though there might be a battleship admiral or a cruiser admiral senior to him in the task group. That was one of the things that Admiral Nimitz got Admiral King to approve. You have to have an aviator as the tactical commander of a carrier task group. You couldn't have someone who didn't understand carrier operations. It needed that knowledge that an aviator had. Once we were embarked in an operation, Admiral Nimitz and his staff would just sit back and watch this.

---

*Vice Admiral Willis A. Lee, Jr., USN, was potentially the commander of the battle line. However, for most of the amphibious operations his fast battleships were split up and integrated into the screens of the carrier task groups.

The Gilberts operation was one of our first operations where we started to bring our aviation power to bear. We were getting enough carriers and air groups so that we could start doing the things that we wanted to do. We were organizing our task groups around the carriers, with the defense of battleships and cruisers and destroyers. After Guadalcanal that was the first time we started landing and taking over these islands.

Q: It was actually the first step towards driving across the Pacific.

Admiral Hedding: It was the first initial step, you might say, in our leap-frogging across the Pacific. It's been well written up.

It was a real tough show for the Marines moving into Tarawa. We learned from that. We thought we had really softened up the islands and that there was nothing left. But we found out that the Japs had just dug in, and when the units came in, they just let them have it. So that was one of the things we learned.

Q: Do you remember what ship you were on at that time?

Admiral Hedding: Yes, we were on the Yorktown as our flagship, and Captain Clark was the skipper.

T. J. Hedding #1 - 47

We had several interesting incidents there. The Liscome Bay, one of the small carriers, a CVE, had been sunk by a Japanese submarine.* Two pilots had no place to land, so they came in when it was dark to land on the Yorktown. One of them missed everything and piled up into our planes toward the barrier and created a tremendous fire. I remember Captain Clark leaning over the navigation bridge, directing the fire fighters and doing a remarkable job to save the ship.

What I was leading up to was how Butch O'Hare was lost.** At that time we didn't have night fighters. The Japanese Bettys would come in just at evening dusk, or just as it was getting dark, and we couldn't do anything about it. They would fly around and drop torpedoes at us, and they were hitting us, too, now and then.

Butch O'Hare was on Admiral Radford's flagship.*** They set up the first real night fighter attempt to get these Bettys. They had a very simple radar on the TBFs.**** The idea was a TBF would go out with two fighters flying

---
*The Japanese submarine I-175 torpedoed and sank the escort carrier Liscome Bay in the predawn darkness on the morning of 24 November 1943, off Makin Island in the Gilberts.
**Lieutenant Commander Edward H. O'Hare, USN, who had been awarded the Medal of Honor for his achievements in early 1942, was shot down and lost the night of 26 November.
***O'Hare was air group commander in the carrier Enterprise (CV-6), Radford's flagship as Commander Task Group 50.2.
****TBF was the designation of the Grumman Avenger torpedo bomber that O'Hare was to guide on; he was flying an F6F Hellcat.

wing on him, and he would pick up a Betty on his radar and bring them up so that the fighters could visually see the Betty. Then they would go in and shoot it down. They took off, O'Hare and his wingman following the TBF. We just don't know what happened, because he never came back. We have no idea.

On the way out of the Gilberts, while we were heading back for Pearl, we got a dispatch from Admiral Nimitz. His intelligence indicated there were a lot of Japanese ships in the Kwajalein Atoll in the Marshalls. Two of the task groups, one with Montgomery and one with Pownall, were ordered to make a raid on Kwajalein. On the way back, we made an end around and came in on Kwajalein from the northeast.* We were very fortunate getting in there undetected. A controversy developed, which was probably one of the reasons why Admiral Pownall was eventually relieved of his command.

One of the air group commanders and I recommended that we make a fighter strike the afternoon before to knock out all the Japanese planes, and then come in the next day with our complete deck loads and really clear up the place. Before we went in, we had a conference on our flagship with Admiral Montgomery. He flew over and landed, and we had this conference. He recommended that we not have the late-

---

*This operation took place on 4 December 1943.

T. J. Hedding #1 - 49

afternoon fighter raid, and Admiral Pownall went along with him.

Q: Why didn't Montgomery want to do that?

Admiral Hedding: At that time we were still not sure of ourselves. I think there was a tendency to be perhaps too conservative. We now know that we could have gotten in there. Unfortunately, there weren't too many Jap ships there. The planes were loaded to sink ships. They went in and made one strike. I wanted to go in and stay all day, but we made only one strike, and then got out. There were a lot of Bettys on the field there that weren't even touched, so that night they worked us over good.

Q: Who wanted to stay all day?

Admiral Hedding: The operations officer, the ship's captain, and I.

The afternoon before, with Admiral Montgomery there, we had already decided that we'd only make one strike, and after that one strike we'd recover and beat it. On the way out, we'd send some diversionary strikes against Wotje and Maloelap, a couple of islands in the chain, because they had some Jap fields there. So we only made the one strike, instead of staying in there all day like we did later on, when we'd just stand and work them over all day long. Later on we got night fighters, and we'd work them over at night.

I think there was a tendency to be rather conservative and a little careful what might happen. We didn't want to have our ships damaged. After the Bettys worked us over that night, we avoided them for a long time. They would try to come down the moon path and silhouette us. Captain Sol Phillips had command of the Oakland, an antiaircraft cruiser.* I told Admiral Pownall, "I want to send the Oakland 5,000 yards down the moon path, so when the planes come by, they can work them over." They came by, they'd shoot, but they didn't hit anything. Shortly before midnight, the Lexington got a torpedo aft on the starboard side, so she limped back to Pearl Harbor.**

As a result of that, there was a lot of discussion about this operation. I think that's the reason they decided they needed someone a little more aggressive than Admiral Pownall. Pownall knew his business, but he just wasn't aggressive enough. At that stage of the game we tended to be a little too conservative.

Q: But Admiral Montgomery had also made the same recommendation.

---
*Captain William K. Phillips, USN.
**The Lexington (CV-16) was hit by a torpedo at 2333 the night of 4 December 1943.

T. J. Hedding #1 - 51

Admiral Hedding: He had a strong voice that convinced Admiral Pownall to not make the preliminary fighter strike the afternoon before, and only make one strike the next morning.

Q: What happened to him?

Admiral Hedding: He stayed around there for a while.

Q: Was he relieved?

Admiral Hedding: No, he wasn't relieved, because he wasn't in overall command of the carriers. So we learned something from that one.

Q: Can you amplify on the incident of Admiral Pownall's relief?

Admiral Hedding: When we got back, we would always have a period of rest. During that time we would plan the next operation. We would get orders from Commander Fifth Fleet. The next operation then, of course, was the occupation of the Marshalls: Kwajalein, and in the northern part of the atoll, then a subsidiary operation at Eniwetok.

As I mentioned before, every morning Admiral Pownall would go over to the commander in chief's conference. This particular morning after the conference they called him in and said that he was to be relieved and sent back to San Diego as Commander Air Force Pacific.*

Admiral Mitscher had been down in Guadalcanal in command of all air forces down there, and had picked up malaria and a few other things.** He was a little bitty shrimp, as you know. He was just real tired, so they sent him back to rest up. They called him back, and he came in January and took over.*** He came there as Commander Carrier Division Three, the administrative title, and took over the carriers.

In late January 1944 we went to the Marshalls campaign. We learned a lot about softening up these islands before we sent the Marines in. We really worked that place over. They developed a tactic called the "Spruance haircut," where we just knocked everything down; there wasn't even a palm tree left. The aviators would work it over. Then the battleships and the cruisers and the destroyers would come in, and we'd just pour all kinds of stuff in there. Then when the troops went in, they had a relatively easy time compared to what they ran into in Tarawa.

---
*This meeting was on 27 December 1943. For details on the shakeup and many other issues dealing with the carrier force, see Clark Reynolds, <u>The Fast Carriers: The Forging of an Air Navy</u> (Annapolis: Naval Institute Press, 1992).
**Rear Admiral Marc A. Mitscher, USN, had earlier served as Commander Air Solomon Islands and then became commander of fleet air units on the West Coast.
***Mitscher arrived and took command on 5 January 1944.

T. J. Hedding #1 - 53

Q: Your job now was chief of staff to Admiral Mitscher?

Admiral Hedding: Yes.

We made the first raid on the Marianas right after Kwajalein. On our way out, instead of coming home, Admiral Nimitz told us to make a raid on the Marianas--to get as much reconnaissance information as we could on the beaches, so that we could do more detailed planning of the final invasion of Saipan, Tinian, and Guam. So that was the first Marianas strike.

Admiral Mitscher always had quite a sense of humor. He wrote up the orders, and he said, "I cannot tell a lie. D-Day is Washington's birthday, the 22nd of February.* We were picked up that night on our run in. That was the first of our raids while I was out there when we were discovered before we got in. So that night the Japanese came out with the Bettys from Saipan, Tinian, and Guam fields. Admiral Mitscher said that we'd been discovered, and we'd fight our way in if we had to because we were going in. And we did.

We were very successful that night in knocking down the Japanese planes. This was the first time our 5-inch influence shells really worked, and we were burning the

---

*This strike was on 22 February 1944 after a run-in the night before.

Japanese good. They were all around the task force. It was just wonderful to see them burning. We got in and worked them over for several days, got a lot of photographs that we needed, and came back.

Q: I know that you had known Admiral Mitscher before. It might be an appropriate time to describe him as you knew him.

Admiral Hedding: I first got to know him when he was assistant chief of the Bureau of Aeronautics under Admiral King. I was in the Bureau of Aeronautics, so I got to know him fairly well.

Then when I reported to the <u>Saratoga</u> for duty, Commander Turner was executive officer. He ran quite an unusual ship; he did everything himself. It got so that the officers of the deck couldn't send a whaleboat in for anything without getting the executive officer's permission.

Then Commander Mitscher came to this ship as executive officer. He gave the officer of the deck permission to send number-three motor launch in or something like that. He hadn't been there very long, and having known me, he called me in and said, "What's going on? What's the matter with my officers of the deck?"

I said, "Do you know who you relieved?"

He said, "Oh."

So he got the senior watch officer to pass the word that he wanted his officer of the deck to run the deck. It was his business and not to bother the exec with all these silly requests as to whether to send number-three motor launch in.

I got to know him real well there, which you do aboard ship. Then the war came along, and I didn't see him until he came out there to take over the fast carriers. He was a great man. Looking back on my naval career, I worked for practically all the top aviators: Admiral King, Admiral Towers, Admiral Sherman, Admiral Mitscher, Admiral Radford. Only two of all the people I worked for do I put in the category of heroes to me. They just epitomized everything that the naval officer should be. Those two were Admiral Nimitz and Admiral Mitscher. They were great people.

I worked for Admiral Radford a lot more than anyone else. I practically spent a career working for Admiral Radford when I became an admiral.

But there was something about these two men; they had a kindness. Now, that sounds funny to say that Admiral Nimitz and Admiral Mitscher were kind people, but they were.

Q: It doesn't sound strange to hear about Admiral Nimitz, but it does sound strange to hear it about Admiral

T. J. Hedding #1 - 56

Mitscher.

Admiral Hedding: But it's true. I've never seen Admiral Mitscher get mad except once the whole time I was with him. He really was boiling that time.

Q: What was that about?

Admiral Hedding: We had a communication officer that pulled a pretty bad boo-boo. We had been making a raid on Palau, and we'd sent Admiral Clark out down south of Truk to work somewhere down near Hollandia. They were coming back, and we got orders from Admiral Nimitz to make another raid on Truk. We set up the plans real quickly in dispatch form. I sent the dispatch in to the communicator and said, "Send this to Admiral Clark right away, because we want to rendezvous tomorrow morning at a certain place." It went out. I thought he put it operational priority, but he didn't. He had it routine.

So we arrived at the rendezvous the next morning, and no Admiral Clark. Admiral Mitscher said, "Well, where is he?"

I said, "I don't know. I'll look at the dispatch board."

I got hold of the communicator and said, "Where is the dispatch we sent to Admiral Clark?"

He said, "It hasn't been sent."

I said, "What's the matter?"

He said, "I put it routine."

I put some fighters in the air and sent them down in the general vicinity where I knew Jock Clark was. They found him and told him what the rendezvous was by voice radio.

Meantime, I told the admiral what had happened. He said, "Well, I want a pound of flesh." That's all he said. That was the end of that communicator. When we got back in, we had him detached and got another one.

When the time came, he could make decisions that were hard to make, that would hurt people. Anyone in command has to do that. Admiral Nimitz did it all the time. If you read this book about how he had to relieve this one and that one and do this and that. Admiral Mitscher had to make the decision that this communicator wasn't working out, so we had to get another one.

Q: You found him kind?

Admiral Hedding: Oh, a very kind man, a very thoughtful man, and a very quiet man. He was a very knowledgeable man, because he'd been a naval aviator for a long, long time. He was one of the old-timers. I just thought they were great people.

T. J. Hedding #1 - 58

Q: That's an exclusive class--to have those two men, Admiral Mitscher and Admiral Nimitz.

Admiral Hedding: In the early phases of our island hopping and raids in the Pacific we used Pearl Harbor as our base to which we returned and refitted. As we were getting farther and farther west, we were losing too much time going back and forth from Pearl Harbor. After we had occupied the Marshalls and the Gilberts, we set up shop in Majuro, a beautiful atoll with a narrow entrance. I think you've seen some pictures of the fleet in Majuro Harbor, just carrier after carrier almost as far as you can see. it was a most impressive sight.

While we were there, we had a lot of fun, the admiral and I. All this time we had to get flight time in to draw our flight pay, which became quite a logistic problem. We were in Majuro, and the admiral said, "Let's go flying." he had to fly too to get his flight time; we all did. That was the rule. To draw your flight pay you had to get so many hours of flying. You could let it run a certain length of time, but then if you lost too much, you'd just lose flight pay.

There was a cruiser astern of us. I got hold of the senior aviator on the cruiser. We went over and got one of the seaplanes. I put the admiral in the rear seat. I hadn't flown a seaplane in a long time. So I said, "Here we go, Admiral," and off we went. We had a lot of fun. We flew all around the atoll there and looked at the fleet. I guess we stayed up a couple of hours. Then we came down and landed and taxied up. It was a lot of fun.

I just hadn't thought about that problem we used to have of getting flight time in, particularly when we moved well forward. When we were coming back to Pearl, we could fly out of Ford Island, down to Hilo, and have lunch. It was great.

Q: That's the first time I've thought of people, no matter what their rank, of having to keep flight time.

Admiral Hedding: I can remember this down at Majuro, and I can remember flying all around there. It was a beautiful atoll.

We set up a recreation island, as we did later on down in Ulithi, when we had a fleet anchorage down there. On one end of this recreation island would be the officers and the other end, the enlisted men. On the officers' side we'd have liquor, and on the enlisted side we'd have just acres of beer. We'd go ashore and play ball and have a great time. It was good relaxation. It allowed us to get off the ship and relax. Of course, that was quite a problem during the war--to have periods of relaxation where

T. J. Hedding #1 - 60

you could just kind of forget about things.

Q: There was no problem of Japanese attacking?

Admiral Hedding: No. At Ulithi they had an occasion where they did a kamikaze deal. They hit the <u>Randolph</u> when everybody was watching the movies in Ulithi lagoon.*

Recreation was a problem. Of course, the air groups would get pretty well beat up, and they would be sent back to the states for leave and recreation and refit and reform so they could come back. Those pilots took a beating more than anyone else.

Q: In an area where there was action, would they fly every day?

Admiral Hedding: Oh, yes. Once we would get control of the air over these islands, then we would get in real close, and fly two or three missions a day. When we were on our way for a raid or an operation on one of these islands, every day we ran combat air patrol and antisubmarine patrol.

Q: So they had to fly whether there was a fighting situation or not.

---
*The <u>Randolph</u> was hit by the kamikaze on 11 March 1945.

Admiral Hedding: Yes. That would come around to a squadron about every third day. They would get a couple hours of patrol or something like that, so it didn't amount to much. Once we got in and started laying the bombs in and everything else, it was different.

Q: We're continuing now with your duty out in the Pacific, and I think we're in the early part of 1944.

Admiral Hedding: In February, Admiral Nimitz directed a carrier strike on the Japanese-held island of Truk.* We didn't know too much about Truk. Everything that we thought about was that it was supposed to be an impregnable fortress in the Pacific, heavily defended. But it was one of those places that had to be knocked out if we were going to continue our island-hopping campaign through the Western Pacific. We also had hopes, from our intelligence and the objectives given us in our orders from Commander in Chief Pacific and Commander Fifth Fleet, that we might find some Japanese ships in the atolls which we would knock off.

So we made our raid on Truk, and again we got in unopposed. We initiated the fighter sweep which we always used when we went in to make sure we'd get control of the air over the objective area. The first strikes were always

---
*Carrier planes attacked Truk on 17-18 February, a few days before the 22 February raid on the Marianas.

T. J. Hedding #1 - 62

more or less massive fighter strikes to clean out the air, which we were able to do at Truk very quickly. We found that Truk was not as impregnable as we had thought, and there weren't too many ships in there.

As I remember, there were some ships that tried to escape to the west, towards Palau. Admiral Spruance in the New Jersey tried, with some cruisers and destroyers, to run them down and have a battle-line engagement, I guess. Strangely enough, I think until the end of the war he was still in hope there would be a battle between the battleships. That was one of the things he wanted to do when the Yamato made her banzai charge down off Okinawa—that maybe the battleships could do something other than lodge shells into some shore establishment.*

It was a very successful operation. We stayed in there a couple of days and cleaned out the place with very minor losses. Then we headed back for Majuro. On the way back, Admiral Mitscher received a message from Admiral Nimitz outlining a new policy regarding task force commanders and their chiefs of staff. The policy was that the task force commander, if he was an aviator, would have non-aviator chief of staff. This policy was approved by Admiral King.

As I remember, the real objective was to insure that

---

*The giant battleship Yamato was sent on essentially a one-way mission in April 1945 to disrupt American landings on Okinawa. She was sunk by Mitscher's carrier planes.

the Fifth Fleet staff had better aviation experience. The chief of staff to Admiral Spruance was an old friend of his, Carl Moore, who was not an aviator.* The only aviator on the staff was a captain, and I don't think he had too much influence on the staff, to ensure proper aviation thinking was used in their estimates of situations or drawing up of plans.

So this dispatch came in, saying that in accordance with this policy, that I would be detached, and he would have a non-aviator chief of staff. Admiral Nimitz submitted four names for his consideration. When I showed it to Admiral Mitscher, I said, "Admiral, it looks like you're going to get a new chief of staff."

He said, "What do you mean?"

I said, "Well, here."

He read it over and said, "I'm not going to do it."

I said, "Admiral, I don't think you have much choice."

He said, "Well, I guess maybe I don't. Do you know any of these people?"

I said, "Yes, I know all of them."

He said, "Okay. They're going to relieve you. You pick one. I don't care who he is. You pick him."

I said, "Okay. Pick Arleigh Burke."**

---
*Captain Charles J. Moore, USN.
**Captain Arleigh A. Burke, USN, later Chief of Naval Operations from 1955 to 1961. His oral history is in the Naval Institute collection.

Q: Do you remember who the other three were?

Admiral Hedding: No, I don't. I think one of them was Roland Smoot.* I just don't remember who the other two were.

I had known Arleigh Burke. We had been at the PG School in Annapolis at the same time. He was taking an ordnance PG, and I was taking aeronautical engineering. So I had known Arleigh. He'd made a fabulous name for himself down in the South Pacific, where he'd been with Halsey.** I told all this to the admiral, and he said, "All right. If that's the one you think it should be, then answer the dispatch and send it in." So I did.

Not to jump ahead, but as I remember, we got back to Majuro to refit and plan for the next operation, which was to be a strike on the Palau Islands, which were still farther west. I'm not sure at that time that any decision had been reached as just where the next island-hopping landing would be. I know there was some consideration for Yap or Ulithi, but we knew that Palau was a strong point in the Western Pacific.

We went in to carry out carrier strikes on this island. I think this was the first time that the carriers

---
*Captain Roland N. Smoot, USN, whose oral history is in the Naval Institute collection.
**Admiral William F. Halsey, Jr., USN, was Commander South Pacific Force.

used mines. We mined the channels into the harbor. We'd never used them before. Normally we didn't think much of mining, because we would rather go in with carriers and knock out everything with bombs, which we thought was a better way of doing it. In any case, we departed from Majuro for Palau.

En route we rendezvoused with some other task group. Along the starboard quarter came a destroyer and a message saying that Captain Burke was arriving. I said, "Admiral, your new chief of staff is about to come aboard."

He said, "Well, that's fine." So I went back to meet him on the fantail of the Lexington, which was our flagship.* Across the highline came Arleigh Burke. He was one of the maddest individuals I've ever seen. he said, "Who is Commander Carrier Division Three anyway? Who is he?"

I said, "Well, it's Admiral Mitscher."

Q: Where did he come from? What had he been doing?

Admiral Hedding: As I remember, he was going to be relieved of his job commanding a desron, known as the Little Beavers.** He was to be ordered back to the States

---
*Captain Burke reported to Mitscher's staff in late March 1944. For an article presenting Burke's viewpoint on the admiral, see, "Admiral Marc Mitscher: A Naval Aviator," U.S. Naval Institute Proceedings, April 1975, 53-63.
**Burke had been serving as Commander Destroyer Squadron 23.

for leave and then put a new squadron of brand-new destroyers in commission, which he thought would be the greatest thing that ever happened to him. He was a wonderful destroyer sailor. To be ordered to a carrier division . . .

I said, "Just relax, Arleigh. You're getting the finest job you could ever get. You'll see." We stopped by my cabin down below and left his things in there, because he could stay in my cabin below. I would still be in the emergency cabin up on the bridge. I said, "Let's go up and meet the admiral," so away we went.

The admiral was sitting there on the bridge like he always did, facing aft, with a little baseball cap on. I said, "Admiral, I'd like to have you meet Arleigh Burke, your new chief of staff."

"Welcome aboard, Burke."

"Glad to be aboard, Admiral." And that was it.

We went down below, and I started talking to him. He was still mad; he didn't want any part of it. He said, "I don't know anything about carriers. Destroyers are my Navy."

I said, "You're about to become knowledgeable about carriers, Chum, whether you like it or not." I explained to him about the setup, why he was reliving me. He couldn't understand why I couldn't stay on and why he couldn't get his destroyer squadron.

He said, "I don't know anything about carriers."

I said, "You'll learn. You've got a wonderful job."

So we went up, and things started moving along slowly. As we started in and got a little closer, we had to call a conference of the task group commanders' chiefs of staff aboard. This was so I could go over our orders and their group orders with them, to explain things and get things straightened out. They all came aboard.

They were flying off, and Admiral Si Ginder's chief of staff, Ken Averill, was in a seat down below in a TBF.* When it was catapulted, it just rared back, spun in, and that was the end of it. They got one of the crew out, but Averill was gone. It sank right away. We were standing out there, and the admiral said, "Well, you'd better go pack."

I said, "What do you mean?"

He said, "You've got to go over and be Si Ginder's chief of staff for this operation. He can't operate alone. We've got everything done, our orders are all written, and we've got Burke here."

So I said, "Fine," and I went down and packed.

I landed aboard Admiral Ginder's flagship and went down to his emergency cabin to see him and told him what

---

*Rear Admiral Samuel P. Ginder, USN, Commander Task Group 58.3. Commander James Kent Averill, USN, killed 3/26/44.

happened. The staff just went to pieces. I said, "Look, we've got to draw up your own op order and get everything squared away here. Let's get going."

He said, "Okay, you do it." I got the operations officer and the communicator and the rest of them. We started writing up the orders and getting the strike plans and everything.

Admiral Ginder wouldn't have any part of it. I would take things to him, and he didn't want to see them. He stayed in his emergency cabin the whole time. He'd never come out. He'd spend all his time writing these stupid daily little newspaper deals that he would get out to the task group. he called it the "Tally-ho Ack-Ack." It was supposed to represent the tally-ho of the aviators and the ack-ack of the antiaircraft. He would tell them a lot of things, and it would just clutter up all the communications and everything else. I knew Admiral Mitscher was just having a fit. I tried to get Admiral Ginder to give it up, but no, every day the "Tally-ho Ack-Ack" would come out.

We went in and got it over and came back. On the way back I said, "Admiral, I'm going back to the flagship with Mitscher."

Q: Before you do that, are you talking about going into Palau? Didn't you just take over at Palau and run the whole show?

Admiral Hedding: Yes, I ran the task group, but anyone could have done that.

Q: You were speaking of doing the planning work for the admiral.

Admiral Hedding: We're talking about planning. I did the plan for Task Force 58. Once they would issue our plan, they would issue their op orders. Then the task group commanders would run their own task groups.

Q: You were doing all this for Admiral Ginder?

Admiral Hedding: When I went over there, I had to draw up the plans and then run the task group.

Q: Can you tell me about the actual operation when you truly ran it? He wasn't even there?

Admiral Hedding: He would come up now and then, but most of the time he wouldn't. I took all the day watches. I had a communicator who was wonderful, and he took the night watches. In the day watches you had to make sure that the strikes went out on time, the task group was turned into the wind, and all that business--in other words, the

T. J. Hedding #1 - 70

tactical command of the task group. Admiral Ginder would come up once in a while and ask how things were going. Normally he wouldn't even budge out of his cabin. He just stayed down there in his skivvies all the time.

Q: Do you understand why?

Admiral Hedding: No, it's written up. I don't know whether he was frightened or what happened, but he just went to pieces.

When I finally got back, Admiral Mitscher said, "What in the world is the matter with Ginder?"

I said, "Admiral, I don't know, but there's something badly wrong with him because he doesn't do anything." And I told him my experience.

He said, "Well, we'll have to get rid of him."

Unfortunately, it had to be done, but those things do happen. I don't know just why. Maybe he was tired. Maybe it was the shock of losing his chief of staff and turning things over. I know with the staff it took a lot of shaking to get them back together again, because they were really a sad bunch. Of course, that can happen. Ken Averill was a very competent person. Maybe he tried to run things too much, and when he wasn't there, everything went to pieces. I'd known Admiral Ginder for many, many years, and I didn't think that would happen, but it did.

Q: Was there anything to comment on in the actual operation at Palau?

Admiral Hedding: No. It was just a normal strike. We sent the fighter sweeps in first to get command of the air, as we always did then. Then we sent the bombers in, and the torpedo planes with some torpedoes if there were any ships. Those were air raids. Raids were primarily for one thing: to knock out their facilities and obtain information. But it wasn't like what we'd do to seize and occupy a place, when you'd go in and stay days on end and soften it up so the Marines could move in.

Q: When did you go into Hollandia?

Admiral Hedding: That came along about two months later, in April and May. That was in support of MacArthur's move up around New Guinea. The Japanese had some airfields in there that we wanted to neutralize, so when they had a landing there they could take over the fields.

Q: Had Arleigh Burke relieved you then?

Admiral Hedding: Yes, Arleigh had relieved me then.

T. J. Hedding #1 - 72

Q: But you were still aboard?

Admiral Hedding: Admiral Mitscher flew back from Majuro with Captain Burke to report to Admiral Nimitz. We had picked up a couple of Japanese pilots out of the water, so they took them back as kind of a sample to give Admiral Nimitz to see the Japanese pilots. I said, "I'll keep the home fires burning."

He'd hardly arrived there when I got this message to report immediately to Pearl. I said, "I'm being detached, I hope!" So I packed everything, put myself on priority two, and away I went to Pearl Harbor. I went in to see Admiral Mitscher and said, ""Well, Admiral, here I am. Where am I going?"

He said, "You're not going anywhere."

I said, "What do you mean?"

He said, "You're going to stay on as deputy chief of staff to plan the Marianas operation. That's a big operation, and we want you to stay here to work with Admiral Spruance's staff and get the Marianas operation planned."

I said, "Okay."

I stayed there for quite a while, and then I got back about the time of the Hollandia operation. We went in for support. That's when Arleigh Burke had his airplane ride off the carrier. We'd gotten control of the air right away, and there was no danger. I suggested to Arleigh, "How about flying in and taking a ride around and see what's going on in there. That'll be fun."

So he hitched a ride in the back seat of a scout bomber with the squadron commander. He went on a typical strike with these bombers, but apparently he got a little lower than he intended, and fragments came up into the wing. So when he got back, he looked kind of funny.

I wrote up this dispatch from Admiral Mitscher to the task force. It said, "The task force commander is pleased to report the safe return of his chief of staff, '31-knot Burke,' from a harrowing flight over enemy territory."*

When he landed back aboard, Captain Burke announced, "I believe the airplane is here to stay." I don't know what Arleigh thought about that, but we did a lot of kidding about it.

After every operation, we would submit a debriefing or comments of how things went, and we would always try to put some humor in it. You needed it out there, because it was pretty serious business. You can't get anywhere in this life without a sense of humor; I'll tell you that.

I mentioned I went back to Pearl with the fleet staff to plan the Marianas. I was told then that would be my final job. I said, "How about getting a carrier, Admiral?"

He said, "We'll see what we can do."

---
*Burke got the nickname because of the high speed at which his destroyers operated.

I came back and said, "How about my carrier?"

The admiral said, "I've got news for you. You're not going to get one."

I said, "What do you mean?"

He said, "You're going to Admiral Nimitz's staff. They want you on the staff. They need somebody there on the staff who'll help with the carrier planning."

So after the Marianas show was over, I got 15 days' leave home, and then went back and reported to Admiral Nimitz's staff.

Q: I want you to tell me in detail about the Marianas.

Admiral Hedding: Of course, that's quite a story.

Q: I know it's been written up many ways, but it's never been written up from your viewpoint.

Admiral Hedding: It's been written up, and there are many comments and many criticisms of Admiral Spruance.

As the thing unfolded, we had made our first raids on the Marianas. The Japanese were not sure if those were just more raids, or whether they were air strikes preliminary to a landing. If they were preliminary to a landing, they had a battle plan which they would execute--

While we were in there making our initial strikes and the amphibious forces were moving in--and actually had made their initial landings--the Japanese fleet was picked up on the way. The major damage done to the fleet at that time was done by the submarines. Two of their carriers were sunk. They had actually gotten their first strikes off at the so-called "Marianas Turkey Shoot."* We knew they were coming.

The night before, we had gotten this intelligence locating the Japanese fleet. It came in when Burke and I were up in flag plot, about 10:00 or 10:30 that night. We got these intelligence messages, and we assumed it was the Japanese fleet. What we wanted to do was go after them. So we got Admiral Mitscher in and went over the plans with him of what we wanted to do--where we would be, when we'd turn west, where we'd be at dawn the next morning to launch our attacks on the Japanese fleet. We prepared a message to Admiral Spruance, who was in our task group on the Indianapolis, his flagship.

We did an unusual thing, which perhaps we shouldn't have done, in forming and writing up this dispatch. Normally you recommend that you do something and give your reasoning. But we phrased the dispatch referring to these

---

*The landing on Saipan was on 15 June 1944. The Japanese sent hundreds of aircraft to attack the invasion forces, and more than 300 were shot down in the "turkey shoot" on 19 June.

intelligence reports. Unless directed otherwise, at 1:00 o'clock we would change course west in order to initiate strikes on the Japanese fleet at dawn the next morning. Arleigh Burke transmitted it to Admiral Spruance's flagship on the TBS.*

We waited around for some time. Finally, we got the answer back from Admiral Spruance saying that in view of certain other intelligence reports, he didn't feel it would be the proper thing to do that. Our primary responsibility was to protect the landings in Saipan, and we should retire to the east. So there went our chances of getting the Japanese fleet. The next morning we knew that we were going to be worked over. We had gotten a lot of other intelligence that they were sending a lot of their shore-based air up through the islands to land on Guam.

They had a considerable tactical advantage in that we were between the Japanese fleet and their bases in the Marianas, particularly Guam. They could launch their planes from their carriers, strike our forces, and then go on in and land at Guam. In other words, they could run a shuttle service. All the time they were launching, they were heading toward us. For us to launch we'd have to turn away from them. So we weren't able to close the distance, and we knew we were going to get it.

All that night the Japanese were flying planes through

---

*TBS was the voice radio circuit, sometimes known as talk between ships.

T. J. Hedding #1 - 77

the island chain into Guam. The first thing the next morning we sent fighters in and cleaned out Guam--the Orote Peninsula and other places. Along about 10:00 that morning we got our first radar contact, the Japanese planes coming in. We had a deck load of planes, so we took the fighters off and flew the bombers and torpedo planes over Guam, to stay over there and bomb, just to clear the decks for the fighters.

So we stayed into the wind, and the fighters would take off and intercept these Japanese planes coming in, knock them down, come in and get more ammunition, and take off again. So that was the "Marianas Turkey Shoot." I don't remember the exact number of planes, but we knocked down somewhere around 375.* In the meantime, the Japanese fleet was having quite a difficult time because their carrier force was attacked by our submarines, and they lost two carriers, the Taiho and Shokaku.

To get back to the decision that Admiral Spruance made--we were very upset about it, Admiral Mitscher particularly. We wanted to get him to argue about it, or try again to convince Admiral Spruance. He said, "No, he's made up his mind, and we'll carry out his orders." Burke and I were so upset about it that we decided that every

---

*On 19 June, the Japanese lost 330 carrier planes and 16 floatplanes. See Samuel Eliot Morison in New Guinea and the Marianas: March 1944-August 1944 (Boston: Little, Brown, 1953), page 320.

year on the 19th of June, no matter where we were, we would get together and cry in our beer. We never did. We've been together on the 19th and remarked about it: "What did you do on the 19th of June this year?"

I think the reason that Admiral Spruance made this decision was that he was not getting sound aviation advice. Art Davis had not reported in at that time; I'm sure of that.* Although he wasn't an aviator, Admiral Spruance had a very good feel for what naval aviation could do. He commanded two of our carriers at Midway in his task group. Midway was the greatest blow the Japanese Navy ever had. I won't say that won the war, but it certainly hastened it because after that their carrier aviation never recovered. So we were able to do just about as we pleased in the Pacific.

We got them the next day. After the "Marianas Turkey Shoot," we got our planes back on board and headed west. The next day, when we were still going west, we sent out search planes. Fairly late in the afternoon we got a contact from one of our scouts reporting the Japanese fleet at some 300 miles, a long ways off. I immediately reported to Admiral Mitscher, and he said, "Launch the deck load strikes and prepare a second load."

I showed the contact report to him and said, "You

---

*Rear Admiral Arthur C. Davis, USN, a naval aviator, became Admiral Spruance's chief of staff on 1 August 1944. This was comparable to surface officer Burke serving as the chief of staff for Mitscher.

T. J. Hedding #1 - 79

know, Admiral, if we go out there now, these planes aren't going to get back until after dark."

He said, "I understand, but launch the deck load strikes." It took a lot of guts to make that decision. No one loved his aviators more than Admiral Mitscher. There was nothing he wouldn't do for them, and they all knew it. We picked up aviators all over the place; we even got them out of the Truk lagoon. He would do anything to get a downed aviator. That's one of the sad things that goes through our minds now. They don't follow that philosophy anymore, and what a horrible thing it is for a poor Navy pilot to be 15 miles off Hainan Island, and they wouldn't go get him.*

We launched a strike and found the Japanese fleet late in the afternoon. Our pilots damaged one carrier. But by that time the major damage had been done by submarines, and the Japanese had had enough, so they beat it. And we never did get them. Of course, when you look at it in retrospect, we achieved our objective. They didn't stop the landings. We knocked down an awful lot of airplanes, from which they never recovered. We could have sunk their ships, and that was the thing we always tried to do. So it's hard to say; Admiral Spruance has been criticized. At the time I certainly was quite critical because we had them right in our hot little hands. We could have really

---
*This is a reference to the Vietnam War, which was in progress at the time of the interview.

clobbered them.

Q: Was there any doubt or any hesitation on Admiral Mitscher's part about turning on the lights when the planes returned?

Admiral Hedding: No. That was another thing--when they were coming back from that flight, he was sitting in flag plot. He didn't even get out on the bridge; he just sat there. I would go into the CIC room.* The radar screens were just covered with emergency IFF.** These kids were lost and trying to find their carriers. The first thing we did was tell them just to land on any carriers. Then we told the carriers to light up.*** We didn't mean for them to do what they actually did, but once the word got out, they just lit up everything, 24-inch searchlights and all. We got most of the kids back.

Q: What had you intended them to do?

Admiral Hedding: The normal landing lights were usually adequate. But the kids were all upset, so turning on all

---
*CIC--combat information center.
**IFF--identification friend or foe, an electronic addition to the radar by which it can pick up signals that indicate which of the airplanes on the scope are friendly ones.
***Turning on the lights on the aircraft carriers made it easier for the pilots to find them, but the risk came from the back that it was also easier for enemy submarines to see where the carriers were.

the lights was a great thing because they were able to find the ships. Of course, they landed on any ship; it didn't make any difference. On some of them they'd take the crew out and push the plane over the ramp until they just couldn't take any more. A lot of them went in the water, 80-some. We recovered all but about 16 pilots and 30 crewmen. There were many that were in the water that night.

Q: You still kept searching the next day?

Admiral Hedding: We combed the water all through there. We sent destroyers. We had no screen then; the destroyers were picking up aviators all over the place. The kids would come by in their rubber boats with the lights flashing and blowing their whistles, and the destroyers were picking them up. The carriers didn't pick them up; the destroyers picked them up. We just kept right on going and used patrol planes for searching the next day. We picked up almost all of them. It was amazing that we could get so many back.

Q: There was no need to ask Admiral Spruance about the lights, though. Admiral Mitscher did that on his own?

T. J. Hedding #1 - 82

Admiral Hedding: Oh, yes.

Q: Then how long did you stay with Admiral Mitscher before you went to Admiral Nimitz's staff?

Admiral Hedding: Until the Marianas show was about over, and it was just a question of staying in there to maintain air cover. I shifted over to one of the transport CVEs. They kept bringing replacement planes and crews out for the big carriers and so on. Then I went back to Majuro, and from there flew on into Pearl Harbor.

T. J. Hedding #2 - 83

Interview Number 2 with Vice Admiral Truman J. Hedding,
U.S. Navy (Retired)

Place: Admiral Hedding's home, Coronado, California

Date: Sunday, 14 March 1971

Interviewer: Etta-Belle Kitchen

Q: Good morning again, Admiral. We had finished our first interview at about the time when you were being detached from Admiral Mitscher's staff and going to Pearl. But I want to ask you to comment on one item. I had read that when Captain Burke reported to Admiral Mitscher's staff that there were long periods before Admiral Mitscher even spoke to him to say, "Good morning." I read that Captain Burke would stand on the bridge with Admiral Mitscher, and the admiral would hardly recognize that he was there. Do you want to comment on that?

Admiral Hedding: Yes, I'd be glad to, because it just isn't so. I realized that the policy implemented by Burke's relieving me as Admiral Mitscher's chief of staff was, to say the least, at the moment not popular with Admiral Mitscher nor Burke. However, when we were on our first raid on Palau and we were assembling the task force, DesRon 23, of which Burke had been the commodore, joined the screen in the task group we were in.

  Captain Burke's flagship came alongside the starboard

quarter, and he came across to the Lexington by highline. I knew he was coming, so when I left the flag bridge I mentioned to Admiral Mitscher, "Admiral, I'm going down to meet your new chief of staff." I don't remember that he said anything; he just looked at me. So I went down. When Burke came across the highline with his gear, I greeted him, and he wasn't very happy. As a matter of fact, he was quite outspoken, saying, "What in hell am I doing here? Who is Commander Carrier Division Three? I don't know anything about carriers."

I remember saying, "Just calm down, Arleigh. Let's go to my cabin with your gear, and let's have a cup of coffee." So we went up in my cabin, sat down, and had a cup of coffee. I explained to Arleigh the policy which this exchange implemented, which I've mentioned before. I said, "Now, even though you say you don't know anything about carriers, you certainly know a lot about the Navy. I'm sure you'll be a tremendous help to Admiral Mitscher in things affecting other than carriers. I also know it won't take you long to learn about carriers."

He still grumbled, because he said that he had been promised to return to the States for a month's leave. Then he was supposed to put in commission a squadron of our newest and most modern destroyers and return to the Pacific, which was what he wanted to do. This change of duty came out of the clear blue sky, and he didn't like it.

I assured him that I thought he was getting the finest job that he could possibly have. We went up, and they greeted each other. It certainly wasn't too friendly at that time. We then went through the Palau operation, and Arleigh began to learn about things: how carriers were handled, the tactical side, also the strategic aspects of carrier operations and things like that. Of course, being the man he is, it didn't take him long to really catch on.

Q: Did Admiral Mitscher ignore him for a long period of time?

Admiral Hedding: No, Admiral Mitscher certainly did not ignore him. He couldn't very well ignore him, because Arleigh and I were just more or less as one as we made recommendations and did things. We always went together to Admiral Mitscher. It wasn't long, within ten days or two weeks, that the admiral remarked to me, "Well, Truman, it looks like this Burke's going to turn out to be real good," or words to that effect.

There was never any real animosity. Admiral Mitscher would certainly not be one to be small enough to do some of the things that he's credited with doing, such as ignoring Burke. He never did then, and he wouldn't do it, because he was a very fine man and a kind man.

Q: Some of the books do indicate this.

Admiral Hedding: Oh, sure, the books love to build up these things. They're just like the press. They like to have bad news on the front page and the good news buried somewhere in column five, somewhere in the back of the paper. Bad news is more readable, or controversy is more readable; it's hard to say. Anyway, they did it in this case. That is not so. And I'm sure if you ever interview Admiral Burke or have interviewed him, you will find that he would say the same thing that I have.*

There was a strained period; neither one of them liked the idea. Later on it became the most wonderful personal and professional relationship that I know of. It became not only a professional thing, but the mutual respect became a personal association. They both just worked wonderfully together. Any idea that there was a period when Admiral Mitscher ignored Burke is just not so.** A lot of naval officers I know could be awful tough and awful hard and sometimes mean. We called a lot of them "sundowners," which is a good old Navy expression. But Admiral Mitscher was not that kind of a person.

---

*Admiral Burke's Naval Institute oral history contains an account of his initial dealings with Mitscher. He says they were strained, but during the Palau operation he asserted himself and then won Mitscher's confidence.
**Admiral Burke said in his oral history of the initial period with Mitscher: " . . . I knew he didn't want me, and he didn't like me, and he wasn't going to say anything to me. He didn't say very much to anybody, anyway, but he certainly wasn't going to talk to me."

Q: Can you describe your detachment from Admiral Mitscher's staff?

Admiral Hedding: First of all, I think I mentioned that Admiral Mitscher flew to Pearl Harbor with Burke and one of the Japanese pilots--a prisoner that we had recovered--for a conference. As he left, I stayed behind, and I said, "Now, Admiral, when you get back to Pearl, be sure and get a command for me, if I'm being detached."

He said, "I'll certainly do it, if I can." A couple of days later, I got this dispatch to report to Pearl to Commander in Chief Pacific. So I packed up everything I had, and away I went.

I got back there and checked in with Admiral Mitscher. I said, "Well, Admiral, here I am. What ship do I get?"

He said, "Well, Truman, I've got bad news for you. You're not going to get a ship. You're going to stay here and be temporarily attached to Admiral Spruance's staff to do the carrier planning for the Marianas operation. When those operations are completed and I detach you, you will report to Admiral Nimitz's staff as the carrier planner in his plans section." So that was that.

I stayed in Pearl attached to Admiral Spruance's staff until his operation plan was drawn up. My primary responsibility was the aviation annex, or that part of his plan that issued the necessary operation orders and instructions to Admiral Mitscher as Commander Fast Carrier Task Force.

Q: Had you worked directly with Admiral Spruance before?

Admiral Hedding: I had before, yes, on other operations.

As I mentioned, one of the problems that we had, and one of the problems that Admiral Towers was quite concerned with, was that Admiral Spruance's staff did not have anyone that really represented modern carrier thinking. I think, from what I've heard and read, that Admiral Towers was instrumental in establishing the policy that required fleet commanders who were not aviators to have an aviator chief of staff. He had only one aviator on his whole staff, and that was Bobby Morris. Captain Morris is a very fine officer, but not a very strong officer. On Admiral Spruance's staff there were very strong non-aviation officers, such as Carl Moore, his chief of staff, and Savvy Forrestel, his operations officer, and others.* That's why Admiral Mitscher insisted that I work with Admiral Spruance in drawing up his operation plans.

Q: Did you have any difficulty?

---
*Captain Emmet P. Forrestel, USN.

Admiral Hedding: No, none whatsoever. There were no problems at all. I worked almost directly with Savvy Forrestel and Carl Moore in drawing up the carrier annex. There were never any problems, because they more or less looked to me as representing Admiral Mitscher. They were just as interested in getting a proper set of instructions and orders as we were to get them. So there was never any problem there.

Their plan was written, and I dashed back to Majuro where the fleet was then. We sat down and drew up the operation plan and operations orders for the fast carrier task forces. When the Marianas operation was over, I was detached on 22 June 1944 and proceeded to report to the Commander in Chief U.S. Pacific Fleet, Admiral Nimitz, for duty on his staff.

Q: Would you break this down into two parts? One would be to describe your functions and how you performed these functions. And the other, as we go through the operations and the actions that occurred in the Pacific while you were on Admiral Nimitz's staff--how much you saw him and how you saw him react to these various things.

Admiral Hedding: On Admiral Nimitz's staff there was a planning group which consisted of a naval aviator; a Marine; an Army logistic officer; a Navy captain who was a non-aviator, more or less for the service force officers; and an Air Corps officer. We were the planners. We worked directly under Admiral Sherman.* And I worked directly under Admiral Sherman, because I accompanied him on many of his trips, such as going down to Brisbane to confer with General MacArthur's staff.** Admiral Sherman had been chief of staff to Admiral Towers, and then he had moved over as number-three naval officer on Admiral Nimitz's staff. There was Admiral Nimitz. His chief of staff was Admiral McMorris.*** Then Admiral Sherman was deputy chief of staff for plans.

In this planning group we were the ones that drew up the commander in chief's plans. Those plans actually originated in Washington, and Admiral Nimitz's instructions to the planners came from Admiral King. Admiral King, working as a member of the Joint Chiefs and also a member of the Combined Chiefs, decisions were made that the next objective for the Pacific Fleet would be so and so. They would write a formal operation plan. We would get it, and we in turn would draw up Admiral Nimitz's plan.

Before that was issued, it would be sent back to Admiral King, and he'd look it over. If there was anything to be done, it would be discussed and decisions made. Then

---

*Rear Admiral Forrest P. Sherman, USN, later Chief of Naval Operations from 1949 to 1951.
**General Douglas MacArthur, USA, Commander Southwest Pacific Area.
***Vice Admiral Charles H. McMorris, USN.

that plan would go out to the Pacific Fleet. There would be parts in there for the fleet command that would conduct the operation, such as the Fifth Fleet or the Third Fleet. There would be further annexes for the service forces and all the necessary forces needed to carry out the operation plan. That was actually what I did there.

The senior people on the staff actually saw Admiral Nimitz every day at the briefing. If he had anything he wanted to ask you, he would have his aide say, "Stop in my office after the briefing."

Normally I worked directly under Admiral Sherman and Admiral McMorris. That was a very interesting relationship between Admiral McMorris and Admiral Sherman. Their personalities were quite different. Admiral Sherman was a very brilliant officer. He had ideas just bubbling out; he was very sound. He would get some ideas, and he would present them to Admiral Nimitz. I attended many of the conferences. Just about the time we'd think we had the plan sold, McMorris would say, "Now, just a minute, Forrest, let's take another look at this." So they would take another look, and he would probably point out something that was very pertinent that should be done. So I considered that Admiral McMorris was primarily a balance wheel on the staff. He wasn't the devil's advocate, but in a way he made sure that things were as he felt Admiral Nimitz wanted. And he certainly knew Admiral Nimitz's mind, and so did Admiral Sherman.

Some reports indicated that Admiral Sherman became increasingly more important than Admiral McMorris, but I never saw any of that. Each one of them had his own field of responsibility and authority, and they worked beautifully on the staff together. The whole staff did, as a matter of fact. On the staff we had Army officers and Air Corps officers. It was a joint staff, and it worked very well.

We'd see Admiral Nimitz all the time. He'd ask us for breakfast, and usually you checked in beforehand and walked two or three miles before breakfast. Both Admiral Nimitz and Admiral Spruance were great health advocates. They kept themselves in excellent physical condition; they exercised. Both of them were the type.

Q: You spoke of going to Brisbane with Admiral Sherman.

Admiral Hedding: That was during the time I was on the staff. At that period the Joint Chiefs had issued instructions to both General MacArthur and Admiral Nimitz for the continuing conduct of their operations, both in the South Pacific and the Central Pacific. In many of General MacArthur's operations the Pacific Fleet had to provide support, both in providing assault shipping and carrier support from the fast carriers.

It was necessary that contact be kept and maintained to make sure that we would do what General MacArthur felt was needed, and what we felt we should do. So I went to Brisbane with Admiral Sherman. At that particular time I didn't meet General MacArthur. I didn't find out until we got to Brisbane that General MacArthur had finally acceded to visit Pearl Harbor. Actually, he wouldn't have done it if the President hadn't ordered him to. That was the time that the President came out to Pearl Harbor. Both Admiral Nimitz and General MacArthur presented their thoughts, their philosophy, their strategic concepts about how the war in the Pacific should follow.*

We continued drawing up the plans. Being there at headquarters certainly was interesting, because you got to know a great deal more about what was going on and how the war was conducted by the commander in chief. Working with those people was certainly a wonderful thing, and I certainly enjoyed it.

I remember one trip that Admiral Sherman and I made to Iwo Jima right after that operation. A good friend of mine was General Mickey Moore, who commanded the Seventh Fighter Command, which had set up on Iwo Jima.** They had, as I remember, P-51s. Their main mission was to fly with B-29s over Japan, to provide fighter cover for them as they went in and out. They had reported that Iwo Jima was secured,

---
*This meeting took place 26-29 July 1944.
**Brigadier General Ernest C. Moore, USA.

so Admiral Sherman and I flew up to Iwo Jima. We decided that we ought to take something up to Mickey Moore; we both liked him very much. So we got a case of Scotch whiskey, half a dozen watermelons, and a Beauty Rest mattress, and took them up to General Moore.

When we got up there, we landed in about the middle of the morning. We found the place in quite an uproar because at dawn that morning the Japanese had come out from their caves down on the west coast of Iwo Jima. They had gotten into the camp of Mickey Moore's pilots and slit the throats of about 15 of them. So it was a rather tense situation. It did help ease the pain a little bit with these presents we gave him. We went around and looked at that place, and I'd never seen a place like that. This was just awful; it even smelled awful. Aside from the smell of all the dead and the sulfur, it was probably the worst place we ever went into, because of the physical aspects of it. Of course, it was secured.

General Erskine took over, and we took General Schmidt and his staff back with us to Guam, because in the meantime the fleet headquarters had moved out to Guam.*

Q: Not too long after you got there was the Leyte incident.

---

*Major General Graves B. Erskine, USMC; Major General Harry Schmidt, USMC.

Admiral Hedding: I'm trying to get the chronology. The Leyte incident came in October of '44. We had drawn up some plans, and Admiral Sherman wanted me to take them to Ulithi, because at that time we had moved our fleet anchorage still further west, from Majuro to Ulithi. The operation was supposed to be reasonably over, and Admiral Halsey was coming back into Ulithi.* Admiral Sherman sent me down with our latest concept of what the Third Fleet would do subsequently, after the Leyte operation.

I got down there, and one of the carriers was in, the Franklin. It had been damaged by a bomb and was in there for repairs.** Captain Leslie Gehres was aboard to relieve Captain Shoemaker.*** Captain Shoemaker didn't want to leave. I know there was a little conflict there.

Usually when I went to these places the first thing I did was to find a carrier and report aboard. I knew that I would always get a good room. It was much better than living in some of the housing that was on these islands. I got there, and I waited. By that time the dispatches were coming out, and you could see that Admiral Halsey wasn't coming back for some time. So I flew back to Pearl Harbor.

---

*By this time Halsey, a four-star admiral, was Commander Third Fleet. In conducting operations he alternated with Admiral Spruance, who was Commander Fifth Fleet.
**The USS Franlin (CV-13) was hit off Samar on 30 October 1944 and reached Ulithi the next day for temporary repairs before returning to the United States.
***Captain Leslie E. Gehres, USN; Captain James M. Shoemaker, USN.

T. J. Hedding #2 - 96

That was after the Leyte show that I went down there, because I happened to be in Pearl Harbor when the Leyte operation actually took place.

Q: Can you describe what happened from your recollection as far as Admiral Nimitz was concerned and the messages and so forth?

Admiral Hedding: We followed that, of course, quite closely, all of that.

Q: Where were you? Can you describe the physical background?

Admiral Hedding: At the headquarters we got the daily briefings every morning. The operations people told us what had happened, so we were always current in what was going on. We also had an operations room where we could go in and see the displays. For this particular incident, which is referred to as the "Battle of Bull's run--Admiral Kurita came through the San Bernardino Straits and attacked the small carriers.* The others came up through Surigao and were knocked off by the Seventh Fleet ships under

---

*"Bull" was Admiral Halsey's nickname. He took Task Force 38 north, chasing after a Japanese carrier force, and left San Bernardino Strait unguarded when Vice Admiral Takeo Kurita and his heavy ships steamed through.

Oldendorf.*

A particular incident, I think, is interesting in that it has to do with what actually happened. Early one morning I was down in the planning section in Admiral Nimitz's underground headquarters when the flash came in from Admiral Sprague that he was being attacked by battleships, cruisers, etc.** I dashed into the operations room. Shortly after I got there, Admiral Nimitz, Admiral McMorris, and Admiral Sherman arrived. They were looking at the board and discussing the situation.

I don't remember exactly whether Admiral Nimitz said, "We'd better send a dispatch to Halsey and find out this or that," or whether Sherman suggested that. Anyway, I was there when Admiral Sherman wrote out the dispatch, "Where is Task Force 34?" Task Force 34, under the Commander Third Fleet operation plan, were the battleships with their screen. What we were concerned about was why Halsey hadn't left the battleships to be prepared to engage Admiral Kurita when he came through the San Bernardino Straits.

I was there when Admiral Sherman wrote this dispatch. Of course, we know the communicators padded dispatches until they were a certain length, and "Where is Task Force 34?" was a very short dispatch. So the padding at the end

---
*Rear Admiral Jesse B. Oldendorf, USN.
**Rear Admiral Clifton A. F. Sprague, USN, was Commander Task Unit 77.4.3, a group of escort carriers.

of it was "The world wonders." It certainly was not intended to be in there, and it was stupid to put it in there.

Of course, you can image the reaction of Admiral Halsey and his staff when they got it. They apparently didn't realize that it was padding. They could have put in so many things, but they couldn't have got a worse wording for padding. They sent the dispatch off. While we were standing around discussing it, Admiral Nimitz turned to me and said, "Truman, what would you have done if you'd been Commander Third Fleet?"

I looked at the admiral and said, "Admiral, you mean me? You're asking me?

He said, "Yes."

I said, "Well, Admiral, I don't know what I would have done, but I know one that I wouldn't have done. I would have never left San Bernardino Strait unguarded."

Because it was easy to have left the battleships or even just one carrier task group there. That would have been adequate, I think, to handle what was left of Admiral Kurita's forces because he had taken a pretty severe mauling the previous day. He'd lost the <u>Musashi</u>, one of the big battleships, of which there were two. And he'd lost a couple of cruisers and destroyers by a severe mauling. As a matter of fact, we know that he turned west for some time and reported to his headquarters.

Later on, when I was on the bomb survey, I asked Admiral Toyoda, who at that time was the Commander in Chief of the Imperial Japanese Navy, about Kurita turning west.* Admiral Toyoda answered, "Yes, he had, but I sent him orders to reverse course and carry out his orders. So after he got himself together, he did go east again."

The thing about it is at that time we knew it, because the <u>Independence</u>, under Captain Eddie Ewen, had a night air group aboard.** Actually, they had fighter planes over that force as they were moving east. Somehow that information seems to have been lost or something in the mess out there. Another thing that was very difficult to understand was why morning searches had not discovered Kurita coming through the San Bernardino Straits.

Among other things, Admiral Nimitz asked me to look into that, which I did. I got all the dispatches, every one that I could get. I did find out that the proper search had not been inaugurated by the small carriers to cover that area. They hadn't covered the exits in San Bernardino Straits for some reason.

Q: Whose responsibility would that have been?

Admiral Hedding: It would have been one of the CVE task

---
*Admiral Soemu Toyoda, IJN, Commander in Chief Combined Fleet.
**Captain Edward C. Ewen, USN, commanding officer of the light carrier <u>Independence</u> (CVL-22).

group commanders. I don't know who it would have been. It might have been Admiral Sprague, or it might have been Admiral Stump. I don't know. Or it may have been directed by Admiral Kinkaid.* I know he was interested because among one of the dispatches he asked if a search had been set up to cover San Bernardino. I know looking over these dispatches that was one thing I came upon--that Kinkaid was concerned.

All these things are a matter of history, and they've been written up by professional historians.

Q: Except you know what happens, Admiral. Sometimes somebody decides to write a book, and they will look at someone else's book without going back to the raw data. That's why I'd like to have you, who were there, tell me as much as you can recall.

Admiral Hedding: That's about as much as I can recall about that part of it.

Q: Did you ever find the message that was sent from Eddie Ewen?

---
*Vice Admiral Thomas C. Kinkaid, USN, Commander Seventh Fleet.

Admiral Hedding: No, but they were over there, and they did find that the night fighters were over their forces.

Another amazing thing about the whole Leyte Gulf affair was that for some reason or other--I guess it must have been more or less a phobia with Admiral Halsey--he was just bound and determined, no matter what happened, he was going to sink the Japanese fleet. He was very concerned about their carriers.

We all knew at that time the Japanese had very little carrier aviation. It was practically nothing. They had never really recovered from Midway, losing the four carriers and their air groups, and from the "Marianas Turkey Shoot." By the time they'd gotten some air groups trained again, they were engaged in the Battle of the Philippine Sea, in which their carrier air groups were just decimated. There was just nothing left of them. They also lost two of their big carriers to submarines. They were even using these battleships that had a little deck aft as a kind of a hermaphrodite carrier.

The planes that attacked Halsey up to the time he headed north were carrier types, yes, but they were operating from fields in the Philippines. They were just not qualified; very few of them did operate from the carriers. They had some on the Shokaku or the Zuikaku. In any case, they had no real carrier aviation, and any one of our carrier task groups could have overwhelmed them. So why he dashed up north, other than that he had that fixation that he was bound and determined that he would defeat the Japanese fleet, I don't know.

Later on, when I was on the bombing survey, when we interviewed Admiral Ozawa and looked into the plans, it was obvious, he said, that he went down as a decoy.* He said he was to lure Halsey north so Kurita could come through the San Bernardino Straits and Admiral Nishimura would come up Surigao Strait.**

Q: What was Admiral Nimitz's demeanor during this period of time when he was in the operations room?

Admiral Hedding: Admiral Nimitz was always very calm. He never got excited. He showed very little emotion. Of course, I was not that intimate with him. If he showed emotion, he probably showed it to Admiral McMorris and Admiral Sherman, because they lived together. I imagine there was a lot of discussion that went on about things over cocktails, and dinner time, and after dinner, while they were pitching horseshoes and other things. When you live closely like that you develop an intimacy.

Admiral Nimitz never showed by his demeanor or in appearance that he was upset or that he was aggravated or mad. He would show that he was very pleased in the

---
*Vice Admiral Jisaburo Ozawa, IJN.
**Vice Admiral Shoji Nishimura, IJN.

T. J. Hedding #2 - 103

briefings when we'd report. When things that were done were very good for us, he would smile and say, "That's great." He had a few expressions that he would use.

Q: Do you recall Admiral Nimitz's reactions during the time of the typhoon Cobra? That would have been in December 1944.

Admiral Hedding: That, again, was one of the sad things that happened to our fleet. Actually, the typhoon did more damage to our fast task force than the Japanese did at Okinawa. Several of our carriers were severely damaged, and I think we lost two or three destroyers.

Q: I wondered if you saw Admiral Nimitz during that period.

Admiral Hedding: No, not particularly. I know that he was very concerned about it and very upset about it, because that is a reflection on your seamanship. That's something that naval officers usually pride themselves on--being good seamen.

It was very difficult to understand taking the task force right into the dangerous semicircle of the typhoon. Of course, a court of inquiry was later set up under

T. J. Hedding #2 - 104

Admiral Hoover, and it attached blame to Admiral Halsey.* I have no personal knowledge, but I have read that Admiral Nimitz felt that Admiral Halsey had suffered enough just in his own mind that he had done this thing that he didn't do anything more. It would have been most difficult to give Admiral Halsey a general court-martial. It was almost inconceivable to do it, because Admiral Halsey was a national hero, and in time of war you don't do that. He was very colorful, he was a great fighter, and he was a great naval officer. There's just no doubts about it.

Of course, he did it again. At another time he took the task force into a typhoon. At that time Admiral Clark and, I think, some other of his task group commanders, recommended certain changes in the fleet course to avoid the typhoon.** But apparently Admiral Halsey put his trust in his own meteorologist and decided against the recommendations. That was June '45, and at that time there was another court of inquiry. The blame again was placed on Admiral Halsey, and also on Admiral Clark. They felt that Clark should perhaps have left the task force, but that wouldn't do either.

As a result of those typhoons and the tremendous damage that was done to the fleet, Admiral Nimitz issued a general overall letter of instructions as to what commanders should do. If he was in command of his ship and

---
*Vice Admiral John H. Hoover, USN.
**Rear Admiral Joseph J. Clark, USN.

felt his ship was being endangered, he should protest and perhaps take the action that he felt was right to do, and the same with a task group commander. That's great, that's fine, but you'd better be right. Because if you do it and you're wrong, and you're more or less in defiance of your superior's orders, you'd better be ready.

I think that covers that aspect of the typhoon business. That was a very serious thing. I know Admiral Nimitz was most concerned. And I have heard that Admiral King practically tore the Navy Department apart about it.

Q: I wondered in these various incidents that happened whether you had personal knowledge of Admiral Nimitz's reaction and comments he made.

Admiral Hedding: I'm sure he made comments that I heard, but I don't remember them. I just have a general impression. Most of my impressions are general, except maybe certain incidents I do remember the specifics, the conversations, the words that were used. But I know it was discussed at great length. It was discussed briefly at our morning briefings when we got the news of what happened, but I'm sure that there were much more serious discussions in Admiral Nimitz's office between these various people.

Q: You went to Guam, you said, with Admiral Nimitz?

Admiral Hedding: I reported at Pearl Harbor in June of '44. Then in January of '45 we moved the headquarters west to Guam. Admiral Nimitz felt he wanted to be closer to the scene of operations.

He always made it a point, no matter where his headquarters was, that any ships that came in, he expected each captain or each flag officer to call on him. They were first to attend the conference and then to call on the admiral afterwards where they could sit down and discuss incidents. This was one of his ways of trying to keep personal touch in what was going on: the attitudes, the reactions, the thoughts of the commanding officers and junior flag officers. It was his one way of feeling the pulse of the people, for it's the people that make things work. That was one of his ways of doing it.

He felt that if he got to Guam he would be closer. If he were back in Pearl, a lot of the ships would never get back as far as Pearl. Then I just think he wanted to feel that he was closer to the scene of operations.

I guess maybe he thought he'd be a little closer to the Southwest Pacific theater, General MacArthur's theater, because he realized that the time was coming when they would have to coordinate their operations and cooperate more and more. There was a continual buildup of the conflict of command philosophies in the Western Pacific, as MacArthur came up north, and we went through the Central

Pacific. There was bound to be, as it did come eventually, a definite conflict of how the final operations of the war would be conducted and who should command who and what. Of course, the decisions there had to go all the way back to the Joint Chiefs.

Q: Where were you quartered when you moved out to Guam?

Admiral Hedding: The Seabees moved out ahead of us and set up a camp on a hill, which I think is now and has been for many years known as CinCPac Hill. They built these seven sets of quarters in a beautiful location overlooking Apra Harbor on the west coast of Guam, just above the village of Agana.

When we first moved out there, however, those quarters for the senior people on the staff had not been completed. Each set of quarters was identical to the others in layout. They had a long lanai or porch, and there was a living room-dining room. Coming back of that there were four bedrooms and baths around an inner patio. Then on one side were the servants' quarters and the kitchen and pantry.

The first thing in connection with our move to Guam is that Admiral Nimitz arranged for all these mess attendants and stewards that were Guamanians to be ordered to Guam so they could see their families that they hadn't seen for a long time. So we had many Guamanian servants, and, of course, I always felt that they were the best.

Those were beautiful quarters. When we first got out there, they were not finished. I think Admiral Nimitz's and the one next door were finished. So we lived in huge double Quonsets, which were not too comfortable. And it was the rainy season. The rainy season in a tropical island is miserable. The humidity is always right up to the top; it's hot and muggy. There was a horrible smell around the place, and we finally found out when the Seabees had been building they'd bulldozed some dead Japs right close to our Quonset, and it started smelling. So they had to dig them out.

Eventually we moved up into these quarters, and they were very nice quarters. The central one was Admiral Nimitz's. He lived there with his aide. He had two guest rooms. Then to the right was another guest house. To the left were Admiral McMorris, Admiral Sherman, and General Leavey.* Then the rest of us were down the way. Then there were the brigadier generals and the senior captains.

It was very nice. We had lots of good food. It was clean. It was a nice way to fight a war if you had to fight one out there. It was very nice, and we had this big complex up there at headquarters.

Q: How many of the operations did you do planning for, all

---

*Major General Edmond Leavey, USA.

of them?

Admiral Hedding: I was in on the planning from the time I reported to the staff until it was all over.

We made several plans because at that time we weren't sure what we were going to do. Actually, the consensus of thinking on Admiral Nimitz's staff was we didn't want to invade the home islands. We felt at that period of time, in late '44 and early '45, Japan was pretty well defeated. We knew their fleet was practically gone, and without a fleet they couldn't bring the resources they needed from the south. They were just slowly dying on the vine. It still would have been tremendously expensive in human lives to actually invade the home islands, and they still had many kamikazes left. I know about that because that was one of the things I personally looked into when I was on the Strategic Bombing Survey after the war was over.

After we got to Okinawa and were able to build airfields there, we felt that the next step would be to go in the mainland of China, near the Chou-shan archipelago, build more airfields, and just bomb Japan to its knees. Of course, at that time very few on the staff, probably not more than two or three or four, knew of the Manhattan Project to develop the atomic bomb. We didn't know about it until it was announced at one morning briefing that an atomic bomb had been dropped on Hiroshima.

There were two plans for the final invasion of the home islands. One was Olympic; that was the one where we'd go into southern Kyushu around Kagoshima Bay. Then eventually we would go into the Kanto Plain, which supposedly would be the final operation. The Kanto Plain is where Tokyo is. The code name for that operation was Coronet.* Fortunately, we didn't have to do it.

By that time we were roaming the Pacific at will. We were attacking what ships they had left in Kure, at their main naval base in the Inland Sea. We were roaming up and down and just doing anything we wanted. Even the battleships were going in and bombing the home islands. So it appeared to us that it would be unacceptable to go in there and lose all the human life. Of course, there were two thing that made it exceedingly difficult. One was the Potsdam unconditional surrender policy.** Second, we felt unless we hurried up and ended the Pacific war, our people would lose their enthusiasm. There had been V-E Day, and Germany had surrendered.*** The Army wanted to rush everything out to the Pacific and win that war, which was already won.

Early in the time there was a question of whether we'd

---
*The invasion of the island of Honshu was scheduled for March 1946.
**The Allied leaders—Truman, Stalin, and Churchill—met at Potsdam, Germany, in late July 1945 to discuss a variety of war-related issues.
***The surrender took place on 7 May 1945 and was announced publicly the following day.

T. J. Hedding #2 - 111

go into Formosa. We didn't want to go into Formosa; that would have been very bloody. Of course, we did get Okinawa, and we were building up fields in there. The next plan that was approved was to go into southern Kyushu, not into the Chinese mainland, which we wanted to do.

Later on, when I was on the bombing survey and interrogated the senior people, one of them was Marquis Kido, who was the Lord Keeper of the Privy Seal. In other words, he was the direct channel from the Imperial War Council to the Emperor. We interrogated him and asked him about it. The Air Corps then wanted to try to build up the thought that the atomic bomb won the war. We knew that wasn't so, because we knew at that time Japan was actually defeated.

Q: What did you think of using the atomic bomb?

Admiral Hedding: It's a weapon, and as long as we have weapons we're going to use them. Only under the circumstances where we feel like there's a deterrent that we will get the same thing back. I don't think it was necessary to use the atomic bomb. Japan was already defeated. But the President made the decision, and it probably saved a great many lives that we would have lost in our final assault on the home islands, because that's what we were going to do.

The Japanese Army felt that they had never been defeated. The Japanese Navy, yes. They knew it; their ships were gone. They had some pilots left, and they were busy with these two-man submarines and other types of kamikaze operations. The army had been defeated piecemeal, on the little island-hopping deal. They'd been defeated in the Philippines, New Guinea, and other places, but they still had a tremendous number of men under arms. They had them in Manchuria, the Chinese mainland, and in the home islands. They had some 5,000 planes that were ready to be used as kamikazes for this final home defense. As we knew, every civilian who could even carry a spear would have fought.

Q: So you feel that it was a weapon that had to be used?

Admiral Hedding: I don't know that it had to be used, but the fact that it was used saved a great many American lives.

Q: Did you ever hear Admiral Nimitz comment on its use?

Admiral Hedding: No. We asked Marquis Kido about that: "Did the atomic bomb win the war or what?"

He said, "No, but what it did do, it got the fence sitters off the fence."

T. J. Hedding #2 - 113

At that stage of the war, Japan was run by a council of six people: the Prime Minister, the Foreign Minister, the Chief of Staff of the Army, the Chief of Staff of the Navy, the Secretary of the Army, and the Secretary of the Navy. Those six people actually made the decisions. Of course, before a major decision could be really implemented, it supposedly had to be approved by the Emperor, so that's where it went through Marquis Kido.

This is a little ahead of myself, but we are talking about the atomic bomb. In our interrogation of Admiral Toyoda, who was the last Commander in Chief of the Imperial Japanese Navy, he told about this final meeting where they could not reach a decision. The Prime Minister, Tojo, the Chief of Staff of the Army, and the Secretary of the Army voted no--not to accept unconditional surrender. The Foreign Minister, the Secretary of the Navy, and the Chief of Staff of the Navy voted yes. The Navy knew they were defeated.

Q: Was that after the bomb had been used?

Admiral Hedding: Yes. They had gotten the word on what the bomb had done, but these three diehards--Tojo and the two Army people--held out. This was then turned over, through Marquis Kido, to the Emperor. The Emperor said he would make the unacceptable decision and accept unconditional surrender. We were interrogating Admiral Toyoda in an office, and I remember he started crying. It was quite an impressive story of what happened. They then decided the Emperor would issue a rescript, go on the radio, and tell the people of Japan that he had decided to surrender.

I don't know how true it is, but the story is that there was a group of very militant young officers who tried to stop the messenger bringing the rescript from the Imperial Palace to the broadcasting station. They didn't want to surrender.

There was a great amount of concern with each of the people we interrogated there. When General MacArthur decided that he would personally land at Atsugi and then go on into Tokyo and establish his headquarters there in the embassy in the downtown office after surrender, they were concerned whether or not they could really control the young militant Army officers. They were afraid that just going from Atsugi on into Tokyo there might be an incident where General MacArthur might be killed, and they were concerned about it. Fortunately, it didn't happen that way.

I think the inherent attitude--taught to them through generations of obedience to the supreme being of the Emperor, was enough to control them. I think it if hadn't been an imperial rescript, it wouldn't have worked.

T. J. Hedding #2 - 115

After me moved out to Guam, the war kept getting more intense. We had more ships in the area; we could do a lot more. Of course, we had the bloody battle for Iwo Jima; following that was the move into Okinawa. That was a very tough one, particularly tough on the Navy. We lost more ships to kamikazes there, except for the big ships. Those picket destroyers on picket stations--that was just something. I was very interested in that part of the operation.

When on the bombing survey we wrote up our brief history of the war, which was the naval section. We called it The Air Campaigns of the Pacific War, which was issued by the bombing survey.* That particular part of the war was mine to write up--the move into Okinawa and the final actions leading up to the surrender. One of the outstanding elements of the Okinawa campaign was the kamikaze attacks on the ships. So I got into that quite thoroughly. It's all written up there.

They were well organized. They would come down the chain of islands to Okinawa in groups of 10 or 15 or 300 or 400 at a time. The pilots were actually very poorly trained. They were able to fly the planes, but they weren't able to navigate very well. So they usually had a leader. The actual navigation was not particularly difficult; they'd just come down the island chain until

---
*Published by the U.S. Strategic Bombing Survey in 1947.

they got to Okinawa. The first ships they'd see would be the destroyers at the northern picket stations, and down they'd come.

At those northern picket stations we had a lot of ships sunk, and we had a lot sunk around Kerama Rhetto. When they would come, they would make smoke and try to cover up the transports and all the other shipping that we had in there and all the damaged shipping, which there was a lot of. The kamikaze is, you might say, traditionally Japanese. The warrior in Japan has always had a leading role, like the Samurai warriors. That develops a military philosophy that the Japanese armed forces had. I was very interested in how you can get these pilots to take off on a kamikaze mission, knowing they were not going to return. The instinct that we all have to keep alive is so strong-- how did they overcome it?

I interrogated one officer, Captain Fuchida.* Captain Fuchida was better known as the commander of the air group that attacked Pearl Harbor. (I think now he's a Baptist minister.) I was interested in how they got all these pilots hopped up to put the white scarves around their heads and get into Bettys with 500-pound bombs slung on them and then go down and just dive into our ships. I asked him, "Did you give them any drugs?"

"No."

---

*Captain Mitsuo Fuchida, IJN.

"How did you do it?"

He said, "It's probably very difficult for you to understand, but to us it's bushido."

"Bushido" in Japanese means the way of the warrior. It goes back to the Samurai tradition. A lot of these kids were just barely able to take off, fly the planes, then dive into our ships.

Q: Of course, they were ordered; they weren't volunteered.

Admiral Hedding: I think most of them were volunteers at the beginning. Later on a squadron commander would volunteer his squadron. So I don't know how many of them actually went down there because they were ordered to, or partly because they were ordered to, or partly because they felt that was what they should do.

But certainly indicative of how they were able to motivate these pilots is the following incident. During the late stages of the war they put the operations of all the kamikazes, including Army and Navy, under Vice Admiral Onishi.* During the interrogations I said, "I would like to see Admiral Onishi and talk to him about this."

They said, "We're so sorry."

I said, "You're so sorry? Why?"

"Well, Admiral Onishi is gone."

---
*Takijiro Onishi, IJN.

T. J. Hedding #2 - 118

I said, "What do you mean he's gone?"

They said, "About 10:00 o'clock in the morning of 15 August, when hostilities were to end at noon, Admiral Onishi put on his number-one uniform, he got in his plane, and he headed for Okinawa."*

I said, "Is that so?"

They said, "Yes, that's so."

So I looked up all our action reports to see if I could find where we shot down a plane about that time. I never did find out for sure whether he'd been shot down. But, anyway, that was the end of Vice Admiral Onishi. I think that is illustrative of what they could do. Here's a vice admiral who gets himself up in his number-one uniform, gets in a plane, and takes off on his "banzai." It can really make you stop and think.

Q: It's a different form of hara-kiri.

Admiral Hedding: Yes. Of course, we ran into that many times. They did it in Guam and in Saipan. They had a lot of these Okinawan people so hopped up they'd push them over the cliffs and things like that.

Q: We want to check on other incidents relating to your association with Admiral Nimitz's staff between now and the

─────────
*Other sources indicate the Onishi died by the traditional hara-kiri method.

end of the war.

Admiral Hedding: Admiral Sherman and I used to take off on planning operations. In one of them we flew from Guam to Okinawa. Fighting was still going on there. In fact, there were still rugged operations as they were pushing the Japanese farther and farther south and also up to the north. Admiral Sherman and I landed in Okinawa and stayed with the Marines on Yontan Field. I stayed as the personal guest of General Pat Mulcahy, who had the Marine air group on Yontan Field.*

I had a brother-in-law, my wife's brother, who was a captain in the Marines. He was somewhere down south in combat operations. I finally found out that he was in an MP company.** So I got a Marine and a Jeep, and I headed for the front lines down on the south end of the island. I got as far as I could and got to the MP camp, where they had a prisoner stockade. I finally found my brother-in-law. As usual, I gave him the traditional bottle of whiskey, which is really something when you're in combat.

We looked all around while I was there and discussed a lot of things, but my main purpose there was to talk with the admiral in command of the Seabees who would be responsible for building airfields we were going to build

---

*Major General Francis P. Mulcahy, USMC, Commander Task Group 99.2.
**MP--military police.

on Okinawa for the final aerial assault. We were bringing in as many air squadrons as we could logistically support. When the war in Europe was over, General Arnold offered all the squadrons they used in Europe to move out to WestPac for support of the final assault of Japan.* Of course, at that time we had the B-29s under General Harmon, who was later lost in a flight between Guam and Hawaii.**

Then General LeMay came out and took over the B-29 operations.*** He made some very drastic changes. I know it's all been written up, but it's very interesting to see what this man did. They had been bombing Japan, supposedly strategic bombing, from around 30,000 feet. They were trying to knock out some of the airplane plants and munition plants and manufacturing plants that supported the war. In spite of some of the publicity, you're not able to put a pickle in a barrel at 30,000 feet. Furthermore, they ran into terrific jet streams, which they didn't know too much about. These were 150-mile-an hour winds that would just stop the planes. They weren't hitting anything.

General LeMay was there for a time, and he changed the whole tactics of using the B-29s. He brought them in

---

*General of the Army Henry H. Arnold, USA, Commanding General of the Army Air Forces, a member of the Joint Chiefs of Staff. WestPac--Western Pacific.
**Lieutenant General Millard F. Harmon, USA, commander of all Army Air Forces units in the Pacific area until his death in February 1945.
***Major General Curtis E. LeMay, USA, commanding general of the XXI Bomber Commander, based on Guam.

between 5,000 and 10,000 feet at night with incendiaries and just burned the place down. He even took defensive armament off the B-29s to carry more incendiaries. I used to go up and watch them take off from Guam. One of my friends out there was General Tommy Power, who later on became SAC commander in Omaha.* We'd go up and watch them take off and try to get up there early in the morning to see them come back.

There was a B-29 incendiary raid on Tokyo in March of 1945. I don't know whether my figures are right, but they're certainly comparable. They got in just at the time there was a high wind and dropped these incendiaries all over Tokyo. Combined with the high wind, I think there were more civilian casualties--or they were comparable--to what the atomic bomb did to Hiroshima. They just burned the place out. When we went in there later on the bombing survey, driving up from Yokohama you could just see mile after mile of rubble. Their houses were wooden. The only things left standing up were the chimneys, little safes, and the little hibachi pots.

There's another incident I don't believe has been written up. We knew that eventually the carriers would be within striking distance of the home islands. I worked together with the Air Corps planner on the staff, and we

---
*Brigadier General Thomas S. Power, USA, one of the three wing commanders under General LeMay. SAC--Strategic Air Command.

also worked with General Harmon back in Pearl before we went west. The idea was that it would be ideal to get carrier support of Air Corps operations. At that time we were doing horizontal bombing from high altitude with poor results. We said, "We will give 1,000 fighter sorties over the Tokyo area, and we will clean out all the defensive fighters. Your bombers can then come in at whatever altitude you want and be able to do some damage.

I remember we had this conference in Admiral Sherman's office on Guam: General LeMay, the Air Corps planner, and myself. The two of us presented our concept of how the carriers could provide fighter sorties over the Tokyo area or over the western part of the Inland Sea or over any particular area. We would provide at least 1,000 fighter sorties a day, and then the B-29s would come in. General LeMay sat there with his cigar. Finally he took his cigar out and said, "I don't care how many fighter sorties you have. All I want is good weather." That ended the conference real quick. I think that's typical of General LeMay and some of the thinking of the Air Corps.

We had another incident, and this was happenstance. The timing was such that we were making a carrier strike on Formosa about the same time that the first B-29s were operating from the mainland of China. They made an attack on Formosa at the same time as the carriers. They had no fighter opposition and were able to do considerable damage.

We used that as an example of what we were talking about, but that ended the discussion with General LeMay. He was quite a character, and they needed somebody like that.

The previous commander, General Hansell, was the first commanding officer of the 21st Bombardment Group.* I think that's what they called the B-29s when they first came to Guam. I do know that he was a Texan. When he first landed at Hickam Field on his way out, Admiral Nimitz went down to see him, because he was also a Texan.** All during the war that attachment he had for Texas came out many times. He would see people and say, "Where are you from, son?"

"Texas."

"Oh," and then he'd stop. "What part of Texas?" And so on. He might even know somebody there, or might even know his family. Admiral Nimitz was a very patriotic Texan.

I think now I'll try to wrap up all the last few months of my duty with Admiral Nimitz on Guam. In all our planning we tried to set up a three-to-one advantage of our amphibious forces over the defenders. Our intelligence indicated that in southern Kyushu there were approximately three divisions of Japanese around Kagoshima Bay. So we set up with Marines and Army some nine divisions with three

---
*Brigadier General Haywood S. Hansell, USA, commanding general of the XII Bomber Command.
**Hickam Field was an Army Air Forces base adjacent to Pearl Harbor in Hawaii.

divisions in reserve, which more or less carried out our three-to-one philosophy which we tried to use all throughout the Pacific.

However, we found out later that instead of three divisions in southern Kyushu, the Japanese had six or seven. So that probably would have been a pretty hard nut to crack, and there would have been many casualties. As I mentioned, we'd have lost a lot of ships to kamikazes, to their two-man submarines, and a lot of other weapons they'd have set up for the defense of the home islands.

During the last stages--I think the last few months of the war--the British came in. When the war was over in Europe, they wanted to participate. So they sent a task group, under a British admiral, to join our task force of fast carriers. It was tactically organized very similar to the way we organized our task groups. However, we did have a problem in logistics, because our logistics didn't meet their requirements. So one of the agreements was that they would also provide their own logistic support for their task group. Then they were assigned missions in our operations.

In the meantime, I had finally talked Admiral McMorris into allowing me to be detached and go home for a little leave, then command a carrier. I'd been fighting for it ever since I'd gotten there. I kept asking him, "Well,

T. J. Hedding #2 - 125

look, why can't I command a carrier? I've got a lot of experience, I've been in carriers all my life, and my classmates are commanding carriers."

Admiral McMorris would say, "Truman, sure you've got a lot of classmates there, and they're very fine captains of carriers. But very few of them have your background of experience that we need here on the staff. So you just shut up and go up and do what you're told to do."

I still kept at him, and finally in July of '45 I got orders. I was to leave around the 13th or 14th of August. A British battleship came to Guam, and they had a ceremony in which Admiral Nimitz was given some outstanding award by the King. It was presented to him by a British admiral. Afterwards they had a dinner party aboard the British battleship.*

I had the command duty, and I was up in headquarters. The communications officer came around and said, "I've got an 'eyes-only' dispatch for the admiral."

I said, "Well, let me see it." We had authority under circumstances like that that you could take a glance at it, particularly if Admiral Nimitz wasn't physically there. So I got it, and it was a message from Admiral King, "eyes only" to Admiral Nimitz, alerting him to a possible surrender. I got an officer and sent him out to the ship

---

*On 10 August, Admiral Sir Bruce Fraser, RN, Commander in Chief of the British Pacific Fleet, presented Nimitz with the Order of Knight Grand Cross of the Bath on board the battleship HMS Duke of York.

T. J. Hedding #2 - 126

to give this to Admiral Nimitz. Sure enough, the surrender came along in a few days.*

In the meantime, I was detached on the 14th and flew into Honolulu. I was actually in Honolulu on my way home when the surrender took place. The surrender ceremonies were to take place later on aboard the battleship Missouri with much pomp and ceremony.**

Q: Were your orders to go to a carrier?

Admiral Hedding: Yes, a carrier.

Q: Did it say which one?

Admiral Hedding: No, it didn't say. It said, "In connection with the fitting out and on board when commissioned." They were turning them out; some were small ones. I hoped to get at least a CVL.

I was home on leave and decided, "I don't want this carrier now; the war's all over." So I got on the phone and called my friend, Captain Johnny Heath, the detail officer in the Bureau of Aeronautics, rather than in BuPers.*** I said, "Johnny, how about changing my orders?"

---

*The Japanese surrendered on 15 August.
**The date of the formal surrender ceremony was 2 September.
***Captain John P. Heath, USN; BuPers--Bureau of Naval Personnel.

He said, "What do you want to do?"

I said, "I don't know. I don't want to command a carrier now and go out there. I fitted out the Essex, and I don't want any part of it. How about a job somewhere in the good old U.S.A.?"

He said, "What?"

I said, "How about heading up the ROTC unit at the University of San Francisco?"*

He said, "Is that really what you want?"

I said, "Yes. I'm fed up with the war. I don't want to have any part of it. I'd like to go up there. I think it would be a nice place to be."

He said, "Okay, we'll do it."

Two days later I got a phone call from him, and he said, "You're going to the Strategic Bombing Survey."

I said, "What is that?"

He said, "It's a group set up by the President. They have just completed a survey of the strategic bombing of Europe. Now they are setting up a similar program for the Strategic Bombing Survey of Japan. Ralph Ofstie is heading up the Navy section and has asked for you, so you are being ordered."

I said, "How soon?"

He said, "Right now."

I said, "Okay." I packed up again and headed for Guam. I got out there and checked in with Ralph Ofstie,

---

*ROTC--reserve officer training corps.

and he said, "Here's what we're going to do."

The staff at that time consisted of me as number two, and a classmate of mine, Captain Teller; Captain Jim Russell, who later became Vice CNO; Courtney Shands, who later became a flag officer; and a young commander by the name of Tom Moorer, who now is the Chairman of the Joint Chiefs of Staff.* Ralph said, "I want you to go up and establish our headquarters. I want you to be the advance man."

I said, "Okay."

He said, "Before you go, you've got to go to the dispensary and get your shots."

I said, "Well, I've had all kinds of shots."

He said, "I won't let you go unless you do."

I went over there and told them where I was going. They said, "Okay, Captain, just sit down."

Pretty soon here came a corpsman with hands full of needles. He said, "Where do you want them?"

I said, "I don't care." So I took all these shots, as I was leaving the next day.

I had been more or less president of the officers' club, and one of the jobs that Admiral McMorris gave me was to get some decent whiskey for our club. The next evening we had kind of a happy hour up there, and all drinks were a

---

*Captain Myron S. Teller, USN; Captain James S. Russell, USN, whose oral history is in the Naval Institute collection; Captain Courtney Shands, USN; Commander Thomas H. Moorer, USN, whose oral history is in the Naval Institute collection.

nickel. There was another officer, a commander named Chick Hayward, who was going up on the same plane with me to Japan.* He had been very active in the atomic bombing development, the Manhattan District. Deak Parsons was the leading Navy one in this project.** Hayward wanted to go up and make a quick survey of Hiroshima and Nagasaki.

We had quite a party at this officers' club. Then afterwards we went to Agana and got in the plane for Tokyo. There was a mixup in these little folded caps we wore. Somehow he had gotten Admiral Ofstie's garrison cap. He had these two stars on the cap and the silver leaf on his collar. While we were standing around there, I noticed everybody looking at him, but I didn't notice it. Finally somebody came up and said, "Sir, we'd like to know--are you an admiral or a commander?"

We got up to Tokyo, and we landed across the bay at Kisarazu Airport.

Q: Would you remember the date?

Admiral Hedding: I had reported to Guam on 20 September after the surrender ceremonies. So this was around the 22nd of September. We landed at this Japanese field in Kisarazu, which is directly across the bay from the naval base at Yokosuka. We wanted to get transportation for two of us into Tokyo. They said they ran a mail run or

---
*Commander John T. Hayward, USN.
**Captain William S. Parsons, USN.

something in there every day in a pickup truck, so we got in the truck. We had our gear with us, and we were all wearing our .45s, because they told us we'd better carry sidearms. The Japanese Army was still demobilizing, and the men were working their way home, and they were afraid there might be an incident. This way it would give us a chance to protect ourselves.

So we went into Tokyo. The driver of this truck was wild. He'd go charging down the narrow Japanese roads and took delight in just scattering people and chickens and everything else. So finally I stopped him. I beat on top of the cabin, got out, and said, "Look, Chum, I've been all through the war without being injured at all. Now slow down or else." This was an American truck, and an American sailor was driving.

We finally got to Tokyo and worked our way around to the Imperial Hotel. I reported in, and we got rooms there.

Q: To whom did you report in this job?

Admiral Hedding: I reported to Ofstie. When we got to Tokyo, there was a liaison set up with General MacArthur's headquarters. The actual housekeeping, running the headquarters of the Strategic Bombing Survey, was done by the Air Corps. We were in the Dai Ichi Building; they gave us a group of rooms up on the seventh floor. The whole

T. J. Hedding #2 - 131

thing was run by the Air Corps.

Q: How many people were on this survey?

Admiral Hedding: The total number, I would imagine, would be around 100. It was under Mr. D'Olier, who was the president of the Prudential Life Insurance Company, but actually he never showed up.* The actual management of the bombing survey was done by Paul Nitze, who has had many jobs, and I guess he still has some important assignment in Washington.**

We got up there, and I stayed at the Imperial Hotel for two or three days, and then they moved us into another hotel where the bombing survey was to be quartered. We were eating at some kind of a mess they set up. They were trying to get the Japanese to cook our C rations and K rations because the Japanese didn't have too much food themselves. This hotel had no heat, and nothing but ice water, and it was awful.

The rest of the Navy groups finally came up to Tokyo. Ralph Ofstie took one look at this thing and said, "This won't do," and he got busy. The Ancon, an amphibious command ship which had been an ex-Panama Lines steamship, was down in Yokohama, commanded by a classmate of mine.***

---
*Franklin D'Olier.
**Paul H. Nitze, who served as Secretary of the Navy, 1963-67, and Deputy Secretary of Defense, 1967-69.
***Captain Wilfred E. Lankenau, USN, was the commanding officer of the USS Ancon (AGC-4).

Ralph had the ship ordered up to Tokyo alongside a dock. The water between Yokohama and Tokyo is not very deep, so my classmate was a little concerned. He pumped out a lot of oil and came up and tied up alongside a dock in Tokyo. We moved aboard, and then we were back in the Navy. These were Navy people. We also took pity on some of the Army group and let them come aboard, and they were most appreciative. Then we set up a little officers' club off the gangway in a building on the dock.* It was most enjoyable, although it was rather difficult at first to get organized.

Strategic bombing--as against tactical bombing--is to hit resources rather than, let us say, airplanes or ships or troops or supporting operations. You go in and hit their sources--their airplane factories, their electric power--just like the bombers did from England over Germany. The ball-bearing factories, the oil fields, all of those things. That's strategic bombing.

Of course, since this was the campaign in which the first atomic bomb was used, it became a very important part of the survey. We wanted to get not only the strategic effects of the two bombs dropped, but to find out as much as possible about the psychological effects on the Japanese and what physical damage was done because they were two different types of bombs. So we were looking at the whole

---
*It was necessary for the club to be on the dock because of the prohibition against drinking alcohol on board ships of the U.S. Navy.

picture of what the bombs had done. The Air Corps Group, of course, tried to build the bombing up.

Q: Who wrote your procedures? This was a new procedure, was it not?

Admiral Hedding: We determined what the naval section would do under Ralph Ofstie, and then we'd take it up to Paul Nitze and say, "Here's what we'd like to do." What we were most interested in was the actual naval campaign. So we decided that we would write a brief history of the naval campaign from our point of view, and it was approved. So we started setting up liaison to try to find out the people to interrogate.

There was an intelligence officer on General MacArthur's staff named Smith-Hutton, a Navy captain, who had been a Japanese language student and a naval attaché.* I went down to see him at General MacArthur's headquarters. He said, "They're going to set up a liaison group so they will make Japanese officers available for us to interrogate."

I said, "That's fine."

In the meantime, one of the young interpreters assigned to the Navy section had been roaming around Tokyo,

---

*Captain Henri Smith-Hutton, USN. He was U.S. naval attaché in Tokyo when the war began in 1941 and was interned for a time before being repatriated to the United States. His oral history is in the Naval Institute collection.

just seeing what he could see. He came in to me and said, "Captain, I think I've found something very interesting."

I said, "Well, what is it?"

He said, "On the outskirts of Tokyo, at Hioshi, is the Japanese Naval War College. I went in there. There were still some Japanese naval officers and enlisted personnel left there. I thought you might be interested in seeing their Naval War College."

I said, "Yes, that sounds very interesting. Let's go."

So we got in a Jeep, and we took off for somewhere in the outskirts of Tokyo. We drove up in front through the gates, and there was a sentry there who saluted. We drove up in front of the administration building, got out, and here came a Japanese Navy captain. I introduced myself, and he introduced himself as Captain T. Ohmae.* He spoke quite a bit of English. I said, "Captain, where you did you learn to speak English as well as you do?"

He said, "I at one time was in the Japanese Embassy in Washington. Come on up in my office and sit down, and we'll have a cup of tea."

So we sat down, and I said, "Who's here, Captain?"

He said, "Our naval headquarters in downtown Tokyo was bombed out, and we moved out here to the Naval War College

---

*Captain Toshikazu Ohmae, IJN. After World War II, he contributed several articles to the U.S. Naval Institute Proceedings on various aspects of Japanese operations.

T. J. Hedding #2 - 135

and set up our headquarters here. There's about six or seven of us left that were in the planning section of the Imperial Japanese Navy headquarters."

I said, "How long are you going to be here?"

He said, "Not too much longer. We're going to be demobilized next week, and we'll all go home."

I said, "That's most interesting."

We started chatting, and he said, "What did you do in the war?"

I said, "Well, I was chief of staff to Admiral Mitscher."

He said, "You were? Well, I was chief of staff to Admiral Ozawa."

I said, "We were on the opposite sides, then, in several of these encounters."

He said, "Yes, we were."

We started chatting like people will, and I learned more about this. I said, "You people have an awful lot of knowledge we'd like to have." He was a little reluctant, and I said, "One of the first things that I think should be understood between us and your people here is that we're in no way connected with any legal aspects of prosecuting anyone for war criminals or anything like that. We're the Navy section, and we're out here to find out as much as we can as to what went on from your point of view of the war."

T. J. Hedding #2 - 136

He said, "That would be very fine."

I asked about how they were living and everything. They were having a pretty tough time. I dashed back to see Ralph Ofstie and told him what I'd found. I said, "I think this would be a gold mine for us."

He said, "I certainly agree. You go down to General Willoughby's and get them to freeze these people."* I went down. I didn't see Willoughby, but I saw somebody else down there. I told them what we wanted to do, and they said they would do it. So they did; they just froze this group of about seven naval officers who were the last of the group. I think there was a rear admiral, two or three captains, and two or three commanders. They said, "They'll stay there as long as you want."

And I said, "That will be fine."

Q: Were they the last group of the Navy Department, so to speak?

Admiral Hedding: The Naval General Staff, the Imperial General Staff. They were just about to be demobilized; all the rest of them had gone.

I immediately went out and told them what had happened. I also brought two or three cases of K rations

---

*Major General Charles A. Willoughby, USA, was head of the intelligence section under MacArthur. MacArthur was by now SCAP--Supreme Commander for the Allied Powers, Japan.

and C rations for them so they would have something to eat. Then we really started to get organized. We had a meeting, and Admiral Ofstie said, "We'll divide this campaign up so and so. Truman, you'll take the first part of it, the initial planning by the Japanese up to Pearl Harbor. From Pearl Harbor Courtney Shands will take this." Then I would take the last months of the war, from the Okinawa campaign on. I had the first part of it and the last part of it.

Q: And this was all related to the interrogation of people?

Admiral Hedding: Yes. This was really assigned to our area of responsibility--interrogate the Japanese in these areas, in these campaigns, part of the campaigns, and then write it up later.

Q: I wasn't sure as to whether the interrogation was a separate segment from the Strategic Bombing Survey.

Admiral Hedding: When we got up there, Paul Nitze got the heads of the various groups together to outline what was to be done. Probably at that time Admiral Ofstie said what he would like--in addition to participating in the overall survey, to have his section also interrogate the Japanese people with the idea of writing a brief summary of the naval campaigns of the Pacific. That was approved.

The bombing survey was actually mostly civilian. The Navy section, I think, was about seven or eight. I think the Army and the Air Corps had just about the same number. But a lot of the others were expert in their fields, like medicine, to find out the medical effects of the bombing. There were people who were experts in fire fighting to determine how the Japanese attempted to fight these tremendous fires which were set by incendiaries. Then there were psychologists, and there were physicists. There was quite a broad spectrum of people to give full coverage of the effects of strategic bombing. There were economists to determine the effect of the bombing on the economy of Japan.

In the Navy section our efforts primarily centered on the naval campaigns. However, Admiral Ofstie designated me to represent the Navy section in what were called the high-level interrogations. By high level they meant people like Prince Konoye, Marquis Kido, Prince Higashikuni--the leaders of Japan.* Admiral Nomura was interrogated; he came at the high-level area.** This was in addition to the interrogations that we conducted with the Japanese naval people that I found out about.

---
*Imperial Prince Naruhiko Higashikuni, Emperor Hirohito's uncle, was Prime Minister from August to October 1945; Prince Fumimaro Konoye, formerly the Prime Minister, was Deputy Prime Minister.
**Retired Admiral Kichisaburo Nomura, IJN, had been Japanese ambassador to the United States at the time of the attack on Pearl Harbor in 1941.

Certain of the Japanese worked with us; Captain Ohmae worked with me. Since I was going to write up the initial planning of the Japanese, when they embarked upon this war, I asked him about it. He broke out the Japanese top secret plans and used them as reference when I questioned him.

Then, as we got deeper into the various campaigns of the Pacific, we were asking more and more specific questions: "What did you do? What was the damage here?" And so on. Of course, we were very interested in the raid on Pearl Harbor--the plans leading up to it and the actual conduct of it. We were also interested in their point of view of the Battle of Midway and the Battle of Coral Sea. All of these naval campaigns we were very interested in-- getting the information from them to see how it compared with our own intelligence and information.

So we would ask these questions, and they would say, "It will take us about two or three days to get the answer."

One of us said, "Why does it take two or three days?"

One of the commanders said, "We've got to go up to a cave up in northern Honshu where we have all our action reports stored."

We said, "Is that so?"

"Yes."

Just before we left, we sent a team up there. There were all these action reports of every Japanese ship and every Japanese air squadron. They were written reports, and they were in boxes. We put them in a couple of boxcars, said nothing to anybody, and brought them down to Tokyo and put them on the Ancon. We didn't say anything to General MacArthur's staff or General Willoughby. They would have seized them, I'm sure. We took them back with us, and they were all microfilmed. Then we sent them back to the Japanese.

Q: Did you go over and get them out of the caves?

Admiral Hedding: No, I didn't go. We sent a team up there with one of our Japanese interpreters.

I was interested in writing up the "banzai charge" of the Yamato, the last attack of the Japanese fleet. That was all they could do because Admiral Toyoda told me later that they didn't have any more fuel oil. They had just enough for the Yamato, one light cruiser, and eight destroyers. They came down through the Bungo Suido heading for Okinawa. Of course, we discovered them right away.*

This is another aside, but it's one of the vignettes. I think it's been written up in other places. Admiral Spruance and his battleships always had in the back of their minds to have a battleship action, where the battleships would be shooting at each other.** The only

---
*The 72,000-ton Yamato, the world's largest battleship, was sunk northeast of Okinawa by American carrier planes on 7 April 1945.
**By this time Spruance was a four-star admiral, serving as Commander Fifth Fleet.

time it was ever done was in the Surigao Straits, the only time old battleships were actually able to have action against Japanese battleships.* We had all these beautiful new battleships, like the New Jersey, and they never fired at another ship. About all they'd ever done was some shore bombardment and antiaircraft protection for the carriers.

Admiral Spruance wanted to let the Yamato come down and have a dozen or so ships line up and sink it, but they lost contact. By the time they discovered it again, I think Admiral Mitscher said, "Do you get it or do I?"

Admiral Spruance said, "You take it," so we took the carriers up and sank it. That was a rather interesting aside--the banzai that the Yamato made.

To get back to our work on the bombing survey in Tokyo, we worked very closely with this group from the Japanese Imperial Headquarters planning staff. In the meantime, we would have these high-level interrogations of these Japanese leaders.

One of them was Prince Konoye, who headed up the Japanese government just before the surrender. We had him down to interrogate him and brought him aboard the Ancon. We thought that would probably be an atmosphere more conducive to his discussing various things. He discussed

---
*The Battle of Surigao Strait was part of the overall Battle of Leyte Gulf in October 1944.

the aspects of final attempts to get a surrender and all that. He didn't say very much because I think you could feel that he felt that this whole business was part of war crime efforts on our part. We tried to assure him that the bombing survey had nothing whatever to do with it, but at the same time he didn't say very much. Shortly thereafter, he committed suicide.*

Then we had this interesting interrogation of Marquis Kido at the strategic bombing headquarters at the Dai Ichi Building in Tokyo. He was the Lord Keeper of the Privy Seal, and he was the go-between for the Emperor and the War Council actually ruling Japan at that time. Japan at that time was ruled by a council of six people. The Imperial Supreme Council, or some such name, consisted of the Prime Minister, Foreign Minister, Navy Minister, Army Minister, Chief of Staff of the Army, and Chief of Staff of the Navy. These were the people that actually were running Japan at that time. Of course, everything that they did was in the name of the Emperor, and Marquis Kido was the go-between.

Their major problem was to terminate the war. They all realized that the war had to be terminated somehow. As we know from history, they made tentative efforts through the Russians to see if they would intervene. They had this thing facing them--the unconditional surrender determined at Potsdam. That was very difficult for them to accept,

---
*Konoye killed himself with poison in December 1945, just before he was to be arrested as a war crimes suspect.

particularly the Army people. The Navy, on the other hand, knew they were defeated. They had visible evidence; they just had no more ships at that time. There was no doubt in their minds that they were licked.

As a matter of fact, to go back to Admiral Yamamoto, who was their commander in chief at the initiation of hostilities, the Japanese Navy was not too eager for a war against the United States.* However, the Army was all gung ho for it. The Army had tremendous control over the Japanese in that the Japanese country was organized in prefectures. Each prefecture was a very strong Army headquarters, and they were pretty much around the country. They were successful in Manchuria and Indochina and China and every place they'd been, so they were all for this war.

Yamamoto told them, and it's been paraphrased somewhat out of context, "If you are going to embark on a war with the United States, you must be prepared to sign the peace in the White House." What he really meant was that it would be a tremendous problem, particularly when we got mobilized to produce the munitions of war. They had to be prepared to go all the way. The Japanese couldn't stop short by saying, "We'll get just so much of the so-called prosperity sphere in Southeast Asia so we can have all the oil, the tin, the iron, and all the resources we need and

---

*Admiral Isoroku Yamamoto, IJN, Commander in Chief Combined Fleet until his death in 1943.

say, 'This is ours; this is our citadel.' That won't work, because they will build up and come at you, and we'll be defeated." That's what he meant.

Getting back to these six people who were running Japan--the Prime Minister, the Army Minister, and the Chief of Staff of the Army would not accept unconditional surrender. In the minds of the Japanese Army officers, the Japanese Army had never been defeated; it was still there. They had been defeated piecemeal on various islands as we island-hopped. They'd been defeated in the Philippines, in the Marianas, on Okinawa, but to their minds just piecemeal. They still had many thousands of well trained and equipped troops available, both in the home islands and in Manchuria. They also had 5,000 planes, Army and Navy, that were being organized as kamikazes. So these three held out. On the other hand, the Foreign Minister, the Navy Minister, and the Chief of Staff of the Navy realized that the war was lost. They were all for accepting this, but they never could agree. Finally, after the atomic bombs were dropped, as Marquis Kido said in our interrogation, that got the fence-sitters off the fence.

So they went to the Emperor and reported their dilemma--that they could not agree. Three said yes, and three said no. So apparently he said, "I will make the decision. I will suffer the unsufferable." I think those were the words reported by Admiral Toyoda, who attended

T. J. Hedding #2 - 145

this. It was rather touching to hear this tough Japanese admiral, who sat there with tears streaming down his cheeks. It was rather an emotional occasion.

So they said they would accept unconditional surrender, and the Emperor would issue a rescript. Some of the young militant Army officers tried to intercept the messenger taking the rescript from the Imperial Palace to the broadcast station where it was broadcast to the people, the Emperor telling the Japanese he would surrender. That was one of the very interesting aspects of the Bombing Survey.

It was also rather pathetic, I would say, to see the attempts of the Air Corps officers to try to substantiate a lot of their claims of victories won and battles won by their forces in the Pacific when the evidence was not there. For instance, in the Battle of Midway the B-17s claimed that they sank so many ships. We found out later they hadn't hit anything. The ships were sunk by our dive-bombers. There was a general named Orvil Anderson, who later on headed up the Air War College at Maxwell Field and got into a considerable amount of trouble by making a lot of fancy claims.* He had tried to build these things up.

There's another incident I think is quite interesting. Along this line, whenever we interrogated a Japanese senior naval officer we always asked the Army or the Air Corps people if they would like to listen in on our

---
*Major General Orvil A. Anderson, USA.

interrogation. We expected the same courtesy from them, and they did. I was asked to participate in the interrogation of a Japanese Army general and, I think, a couple of Navy admirals. The interrogation supposedly was to be conducted by General Anderson. When I got there, at that time I was wearing an Army uniform. They issued us these Eisenhower jackets and Army uniforms. I had silver eagles on my shoulders, and the only thing that indicated that I was a naval officer was my Navy wings. So I sat in there.

The one actually conducting this interrogation was Major Seversky, who was quite an outspoken advocate of air power, particularly land-based strategic air power.* He was interrogating these Japanese. His idea of interrogating was to expound his theories and philosophy of air power and turn to the Japanese and say, "Isn't that so?"

It's rather amusing that in interrogating Japanese, even though we had some very good interpreters, by the time you put your question into Japanese and the Japanese got it, thought it over, and then spoke, it came back to you quite often with no relationship to the original question. We did find that one of our big problems was to get across not only the words but also the intent of the question.

---
*Major Alexander de Seversky, a native of Russia, was an officer in the Army Air Forces Reserve. He was the author of the book <u>Victory Through Air Power</u>, which became a movie in 1943.

T. J. Hedding #2 - 147

This particular morning these Navy admirals and this general just looked at him, and they didn't know what to say. He'd asked them, "Isn't that so?" I didn't say a word. Finally he asked General Anderson who this fellow sitting over there was, and he said who I was. That just about ended the interrogation. But it was amusing.

I actually felt sorry for some of these Air Corps people out there who tried to establish these things. And the facts of the matter were that their claims were just not substantiated. We know that the reports of damage made by pilots who come back are always exaggerated. They're all hopped up psychologically. It happens on both sides. I don't know how many times the Japanese claimed they sank Admiral Mitscher's flagship and at least ten of the carriers. Our pilots made some claims that later on were not substantiated. That's just the nature of the game.

Some of these interrogations were rather sad.

Q: Do you remember how many people you interrogated?

Admiral Hedding: We have the list of all the interrogations. They are in the bombing survey reports: who interrogated whom. Actually they are all the questions and answers right down the line. That's a good source of information for you, the bombing survey documents. They're available in Washington.

T. J. Hedding #2 - 148

Actually, I'm hitting the highlights, which is probably more important than the specific questions. There were a lot of questions that went on there. They were certainly very illustrative of the psychology of the Japanese. Many mistakes were made on both sides.

In one particular thing it was Captain Ohmae we were interrogating. He had been chief of staff of the forces from Rabaul before he went with Mikawa on the Battle of Savo Island, where the Japanese cruisers came down at night when we were landing at Guadalcanal.* We had all these transports and amphibious ships around there. The Japanese orders were to make a sweep around Savo Island and then return to Rabaul. As they came down there, they made the sweep, but they went right through our cruisers and sank four of them. The amphibious force then was absolutely helpless. All the Japanese had to do was turn south, and they could have slaughtered us. But they made this sweep around Savo Island and then turned north.

I questioned Captain Ohmae about that. I said, "Isn't that kind of indicative of failure in command? Apparently you believe in almost blind obedience to orders. Isn't the local commander authorized to make tactical decisions on the spot?" He didn't have too much to say about that,

---

*Vice Admiral Gunichi Mikawa, IJN, Commander Eighth Fleet. Ohmae covered the Japanese version of this battle in an article that appeared in the Proceedings in December 1957.

except that that's exactly what they did.

Another interrogation along that line brings this out. In 1944 Ralph Ofstie had just made flag rank and was to be assigned to command a group of escort carriers; we called them CVEs. He happened to be riding with Admiral Sprague's outfit when they were attacked by Admiral Kurita's fleet who came through San Bernardino Strait. Admiral Ofstie was most interested. I was in on it, but he personally conducted the interrogation of Admiral Kurita.

Again, we couldn't understand why. The only force actually opposing Kurita with battleships and heavy cruisers and light cruisers and destroyers were these little Kaiser carriers. He could have come right down into Leyte Gulf; it would have really been something. He'd been pretty badly mauled the day before. He'd lost the Musashi, another battleship, and a couple of heavy cruisers and some destroyers. It looked like he tried to go west, and he was told by Admiral Toyoda to go on and do what he was told to do. So he exited from San Bernardino Straits just about daybreak.

They had only visual sightings. At that time the Japanese had no air cover because we'd wiped out practically all their air in the Philippines. He was supposed to get cover from the Japanese land-based aviation, and they were pretty well decimated the day before and prior to that. So when he actually exited from

T. J. Hedding #2 - 150

San Bernardino, he had no air cover, and he had no search. Every time a search plane would take off, it would get shot down. The only ones he had were some battleship-based ones, and I think they were shot down the day before.

So the first thing Admiral Kurita saw visually were two or three of these CVEs, and I think he assumed that they were our big carriers. The wind out there at that time was from the northeast. He knew that the carriers had to turn into the wind to launch planes. So if he could place his force of battleships, cruisers, and destroyers up north, upwind from these carriers, he would really have them, because they'd have to come to him. That's more or less like they used to say in the days of the old sailing ships, "the weather gauge."

So he kept trying to ease around. Our carriers would launch planes, and they would head south. He was trying to get up northeast of them, and he kept going. Some of his ships were hit and damaged. This thing went on until about 9:00 o'clock or 9:30, and by that time his forces were pretty well scattered. They hadn't stayed together, hadn't concentrated.

He had heard the clear language broadcast of Admiral Sprague asking for help, and he knew if the fast carriers weren't there, they'd be there soon. Along about 9:30 he decided he'd had enough of this, so he got his forces together and headed back through the San Bernardino Straits and got clear. In the meantime, Halsey had gone up north.

Q: There was one task group down fueling that did send some planes.

Admiral Hedding: Admiral McCain had been put in charge of a task group in preliminary training to relieve Admiral Mitscher as commander of the fast carrier task force.* His task group had been ordered back to Ulithi to refuel and refit, because they felt the thing was just about over. He was on his way back to Ulithi when the thing happened that morning; then Halsey ordered him to return. He got in rather late because he'd gone the other way. I think he had to refuel some of his destroyers and then came back in and had one strike maybe before they got away.

Q: I wondered if Admiral Kurita made any comment about seeing that type plane which came from a large carrier.

Admiral Hedding: The planes were the same. We had fighters on the little carriers, the same kind of fighters we had on the big carriers. We had the TBFs, which were the same kind of bombers, but we didn't have any scout planes on the little carriers. All they had were the TBFs and the fighters, but they were the same type of carrier

---
*Vice Admiral John S. McCain, USN, Commander Task Group 38.1, embarked in the USS Wasp (CV-18).

T. J. Hedding #2 - 152

planes. So you can't tell by the type of plane whether they came from a big carrier or a little carrier.

Q: Did he indicate whether he knew that he had tangled with the small carriers or the big carriers?

Admiral Hedding: I don't think he ever realized it. Or if he did realize it, he didn't admit it in this interrogation. He said that his forces were so scattered and that he knew since his whereabouts was known, he'd soon be under heavy attack by our fast carriers, even if they weren't these. So he decided to get out of there. He expected an attack at any time. He'd been pretty badly mauled the day before, and he was quite apprehensive, I'm sure.

Q: He had defeated them, and he could have gone on into Leyte.

Admiral Hedding: He could have done that. That's the same thinking that I mentioned, that the Japanese hate to make tactical decisions on the spot. But that's what happened. That was one of the incidents that was very interesting in our series of interrogations.

We finally completed our interrogations and departed on the Ancon and came back to San Francisco at Christmas

T. J. Hedding #2 - 153

time '45. We had leave and then reported to Washington, where we had offices set up in the old Main Navy, across the Reflecting Pool.*

Q: I think you said that you found out that they had in reserve a large number of planes and pilots to act as kamikazes.

Admiral Hedding: Yes. They had been organized into a kamikaze operation. This was the only time, I think, in this campaign that the Japanese Army and the Navy entered into a joint operation. They put all their kamikazes under this Vice Admiral Onishi. He's the one who committed suicide.

Q: I wondered if you had found out anything more. You had said that you tried to find out what the mental state of men would be who would volunteer.

Admiral Hedding: We interrogated Captain Fuchida, because he was one of the primary organizers of the kamikazes. It first started in the Philippines; more or less one squadron volunteered. They found that the effects were so devastating that it was their principal weapon in Okinawa.

---
*Main Navy was the headquarters for the Navy Department on Constitution Avenue in Washington, D.C. The Navy didn't move to the Pentagon until later.

T. J. Hedding #2 - 154

They sank a lot of our ships. They sank carriers, and they damaged carriers.

Of course, the baka bomb that they developed never did turn out to be anything. The baka bomb was actually just a flying bomb; it was only about 12 feet long. It was jet powered and had small elementary wings. We got into Yokosuka, and there was a little airfield right up north of there where they built these baka bombs. They would put young Watanabe in the bomb for terminal guidance. They would hang them on a Betty bomber or something, and they would take off for Okinawa. When they'd get within range, they'd release this guy. He'd fire up his rocket and supposedly guide it into a ship. As I remember, there were only one or two instances where these baka bombs ever hit a ship. Most of the so-called mother planes were shot down with the poor baka bomb guy still hanging on underneath.

We came back from the bombing survey and went to Washington in January and wrote up the Air Campaigns of the Pacific War. That took almost into March. Then I got orders to command the naval air station at Kahului on Maui.

Q: At what point in the Pacific war did you realize that that was number two in importance to the European theater?

Admiral Hedding: That was early in the war. The decision was made, and we in the Navy knew that the first thing was to defeat Germany. Even after Pearl Harbor, until we could build up our naval resources, we were to try to hold the line. Of course, Admiral King was a very strong voice in the Joint Chiefs. Between him and Leahy, President Roosevelt, let us say, favored the Navy a little bit.* Admiral King was able to divert a lot of the naval resources needed to prosecute the war in the Pacific--much better than I think Admiral Nimitz had hoped he would get.

Q: Did it bother you to realize that the war you were fighting and dying for was number two?

Admiral Hedding: We didn't think about it. Our whole effort was to do what we had to do. When we first got out there, it was just to hold on. When I went out on the Essex, I think there were only two carriers left. So all we were doing was trying to hold what we had.

Q: But it didn't bother you to know that priority number one was Europe?

Admiral Hedding: No, you were too busy doing the things you had to do. That high-level business didn't bother you too much out there.

---

*Admiral William Leahy, USN (Ret.), was chief of staff to President Roosevelt in FDR's role of commander in chief of the Army and Navy.

There's another incident that came up during our bombing survey that we didn't know about. The Japanese built these three huge battleships--the Yamato, the Musashi, and the Shinano. After Midway, when they lost four carriers, they used the hull of the Shinano for a carrier. It was a big carrier, and it was built using the battleship hull in the navy yard at Yokosuka. It's the same idea that we used. The Saratoga and the Lexington were converted battle cruisers.

In any event, being built in Yokosuka, they had to get the carrier around outside of Tokyo and back into the Inland Sea, where the carrier would be safe. So she was well along in building when they decided to move her to the Inland Sea. As they were moving her, they had a great many shipyard workers aboard.

They were apparently rather careless in their watertight integrity. They didn't have everything buttoned up tight as they dashed around to go into the Inland Sea. So when they were heading for the Inland Sea, one of our submarines saw this ship. They didn't know what it was, but it was a big one. It was hit with two torpedoes, and that was the end of the Shinano.* Here was this tremendously big carrier that had never had a plane land on

---

*The submarine was the USS Archerfish (SS-311), which sank the large carrier on 28 November 1944. For a book-length account by the skipper of the U.S. submarine, see Joseph E. Enright, Shinano! The Sinking of Japan's Secret Supership (New York: St. Martin's, 1987).

it. They were really upset about that. Of course, they lost a lot of people. A lot of navy yard workers went down with the ship.

We didn't know about that. We knew we'd sunk a ship. This submarine captain reported firing at a large ship, hearing explosions and breaking-up sounds and all that that they usually reported which indicated that some big ship had been torpedoed and sunk. But we didn't know what it was.

I was detached on the 17th of March from the bombing survey and reported to Maui on the 13th of April. On the first of April a tremendous tidal wave hit the Hawaiian Islands, and the captain's quarters at Maui were damaged to some extent. However, the executive officer, who had been acting as commanding officer, had gotten them pretty well repaired before we actually arrived. When we got there, the quarters were very nice; actually they were beautiful quarters.

When the Navy took over this area there on Maui during the war, they built an air station for the training of air groups that were being moved forward. The area they bought was in cane fields, all down to the beach. They got several beautiful homes on the beach. One of them became the commanding officer's quarters, and the other became the officers' club. When the tidal wave hit on the first of

T. J. Hedding #2 - 158

April, it just moved the officers' club back about 200 yards. There was just nothing left of it. The commanding officer's quarters were not damaged too badly, so when we got out there it was very nice.

Of course, that year on Maui--which was just what the doctor ordered, you might say--was a year in paradise. I was there with my family and enjoyed very lovely and gracious living in a beautiful home. We had servants. There are wonderful people in the islands, particularly on Maui. We just enjoyed it thoroughly; it was a wonderful year.

Q: What was the objective? What was the purpose of having a year stationed there on Maui?

Admiral Hedding: As I mentioned just previously, we had these two air stations on Maui to use for forward training of air groups before they deployed on the carriers out in the Western Pacific. At the end of the war they were going to close up the air stations. They had already closed up one, and they were going to close up the other.

I received orders, much to my surprise, to report for duty on the Navy General board. I was still a captain, a rather junior captain. I just couldn't understand what they meant, because the Navy General Board for many, many years was composed of a group of senior admirals who just before retirement were ordered to it. From their background of experience and maturity, they were advisers to the Secretary of the Navy on whatever he asked them to advise him on. Among other things, they were the principal advisers on ships' characteristics--what ships should be like and so on. I couldn't understand being ordered there as a junior captain, but they were my orders. I proceeded to Washington and reported on the seventh of April to Admiral Towers, the chairman of the General Board.*

Things started to fall in place. As I checked in there, I said to the chief clerk, "I have orders to report to the General Board. I don't know; it doesn't seem right that I'm a member of the General Board."

He said, "Yes, Captain, that's what you are. I'll show you your office." We went down the corridor. At that time the General Board was on the second deck of the seventh wing of the old Main Navy. He took me down to a great big office. In one corner was a massive roll-top desk, solid oak, and a big chair with a leather back.

I said, "My goodness, what is that?"

"Well, Captain, that's your desk."

I said, "Oh, it can't be."

He said, "In case you don't know it, that was Admiral Dewey's desk when he was a member of the Navy General

---

*Admiral John H. Towers, USN, chaired the board from March of 1947 until his retirement in December of that year.

Board."*

I said, "Is that so?"

I went in to check in with Admiral Towers. I told him that I was somewhat surprised to get orders to report to the Navy General Board.

He said, "Well, I understand. I was about to retire when Mr. Forrestal asked me to head up the General Board with the objective of reviewing the shore establishment, with the idea of getting a better balance between the shore establishment and the fleet."**

When the war was over, we were busily engaged in the Magic Carpet of getting everyone home, and then secondly in retiring as many ships as we could. The funding was such that we had to do something, so they started putting ships out of commission. It became an improper balance. In other words, the shore establishment was way too much for the fleet, and the fleet was suffering. Whenever you try to close up any of the shore establishment, you immediately run into political implications. The local congressmen get all upset because you want to close a shipyard in their district, or a naval air station or an Army depot, or something.

So Mr. Forrestal asked him to head up the Navy General Board with this primary job--to survey and review the shore

---

*Admiral of the Navy George Dewey, hero of the Battle of Manila Bay in 1898, became president of the General Board in 1900 and headed it until his death in 1917.
**James V. Forrestal was Secretary of the Navy from 1944 until 1947, when he became the first Secretary of Defense.

establishment with the idea of recommending those activities that could be closed out and thus keep the fleet and shore establishment in better balance. Admiral Towers said, "Yes, I'll take it if you let me select the members of the board," and Mr. Forrestal apparently said yes. So he headed up the Navy General Board. Number two was Admiral Soc McMorris, whom I had worked with before, Admiral Bellinger, Admiral Swede Momsen, the submariner; Savvy Huffman, a captain.* There were also Captain Arleigh Burke and Colonel Rand Pate, and the junior member was Captain Hedding.** As you know, Burke became CNO, and Pate became Commandant of the Marine Corps. So it was quite an outfit. We had a lot of interesting incidents and worked hard.

Q: Were there any old ready-to-go-out-to-pasture admirals?

Admiral Hedding: No, they were all gone. So I was the most junior officer who'd ever been a member of the Navy General Board.

I sat behind my desk there, Admiral Dewey's desk, and I noticed two or three times I'd hear giggling and snickering. I'd look up real quick and see a couple of heads pull back. My office was right next to Admiral

---
*Vice Admiral Patrick N. L. Bellinger; Rear Admiral Charles B. Momsen, USN; Captain Leon J. Huffman, USN.
**Colonel Randolph M. Pate, USN.

Towers's. He'd have people come in to see him, and he'd say, "I want to show you something." I found this out later when I questioned him. They'd peek around the corner, and he'd say, "That's a very junior aviator sitting behind Admiral Dewey's desk. I wonder what he would think about that."

I said, "Admiral, you've had your fun. Let's stop this and send this desk down to the Naval Academy Museum," which we did. So Admiral Dewey's desk is now supposedly at the Naval Academy Museum.

We surveyed the shore establishment. Each of us was given certain areas. I had all the naval air bases and naval air stations--the aviation organization. We made a very thorough study of it and made some good recommendations. Unfortunately, they were not able to be carried out at that time because of the political implications.

By that time Admiral Fred Boone came along and relieved me.* I was ordered to the National War College, which was a very interesting year. They had supposedly the top people in the captains and colonels rank from the Army, the Air Force, and the Navy. It was in its second year. Admiral Harry Hill was the commandant of the National War College.**

---
*Rear Admiral Walter F. Boone, USN.
**Vice Admiral Harry W. Hill, USN, served as commandant from 1946 to 1949. During that time the name was changed from Army-Navy Staff College to National War College.

T. J. Hedding #2 - 163

It was a most interesting period. We had people from the State Department. We also had representatives from Canada and Great Britain, and that was the last year they attended. The reason was, I was told later, that the French were upset. They thought they should also attend, but we knew that anything secret or confidential that the French knew or heard about, the Russians had it right away. So the decision was made that we wouldn't take the French. Therefore, we had to do away with the British and the Canadians. They were then all allowed to go to the Armed Forces Staff College in Norfolk. I will say that the British and the Canadians certainly added a great deal to our deliberations and our discussions at the war college, because I'm sure that both of these countries picked out outstanding people to send. We had a Navy captain and Army brigadier, and an air commodore from both Great Britain and Canada.

It was very educational and interesting. Certainly they had outstanding speakers there and an outstanding faculty. I think these joint colleges that we have are a very fine thing, because you learn in discussions with your opposite numbers in the Air Force and the Army that there are other points of view.

Q: You associated with the best of all the services.

Admiral Hedding: Supposedly. I've looked over the registry I get of the graduates of my class; practically all of them made flag or general rank. It was supposed to be a select group of officers. Getting together and working in symposiums and groups discussing strategic and other problems was most educational. I enjoyed it thoroughly.

Then I was ordered to command the Valley Forge, an Essex-type carrier.* After many years I finally got my command, which I certainly enjoyed thoroughly. I think if you scratch any naval officer under the skin--I don't care what his specialty is--you will find he's a boat steerer at heart. There's really no other job that compares to being the captain of a big ship. Because you can stand up there and say, "Right 20 degrees rudder," and it goes right. You don't have to ask anybody.

I was very fortunate to command a very fine ship which had won the Battle Efficiency Pennant the year before. It was called the "meatball." The year I had it, she also won it again for the second time. To me that was a very successful tour, one year.

---

*The USS Valley Forge (CV-45) was commissioned 3 November 1946. She had a standard displacement of 36,380 tons, was 888 feet long, 93 feet in the beam, and had a draft of 29 feet. She had a top speed of 32.7 knots and could operate approximately 80 aircraft.

Q: Where did you operate?

Admiral Hedding: In the Pacific. We were home-ported at Alameda. It was a very interesting year. Of course, you only had it a year, and then you were on your way. I was then ordered to the Joint Staff in Washington.

Q: Were you under way most of the time?

Admiral Hedding: No, not as much as ships are under way now, though we were under way quite a bit. You were able to be home a lot more than the kids are today, in that we didn't have any eight-month deployment or things like that they have now with the Vietnam War. It was one of the things that you look forward to all your career--to command a ship. I did, and I enjoyed it thoroughly.

I was ordered to the Joint Staff and was assigned to the Strategic Planning Group on what we called the "Rainbow Team," the atomic energy team. That team was concerned with the planning on the Joint Staff level for anything having to do with the atom bomb. That included the planning for the use of the atom bomb, any policy matters connected with inter-service business, with the assignment of atomic forces, and things like that.

It was most interesting, and I enjoyed it. Again, it's part of every officer's required duty--to have joint duty at one time or other, in addition to attending one of the joint schools. In this way you can learn that there are other points of view. I think that's one of the things you strive for in the Joint Staff--to get all points of view, not only just the Navy but the Army and the Air Force--the whole bag. Then you can arrive at a proper decision.

Q: While you were on that tour the Korean War started. Did that affect any of your deliberations?

Admiral Hedding: Not particularly. The Joint Staff was not concerned, at least the way it was organized at that time, in operational matters. Later on the Joint Staff was reorganized to have an operational section.

The war was on, but we were primarily concerned in the planning that was done by the Joint Staff. There were three basic plans that we were always concerned in. One was the emergency plan that would be implemented in case of a war. Then there was a strategic objectives plan; that was the plan which set forth the objectives we should try to achieve over a period of more than five to ten years. Then there was a joint long-range plan, which went well into the future, where you try to determine the types of weapons you have and the basic concepts of strategy. These were all strategic plans, not tactical plans.

It was most interesting, and I got to know a lot of Army and Air Force officers.

Q: Did you actually make any plans for the use of atomic weapons?

Admiral Hedding: Atomic weapons were part of our arsenal. There were plans to use the weapons, under whatever circumstances the President would decide, because only he could make the decision to use the atomic weapon. But the plans were there.

Basically, all our war plans were pointed towards Russia; that was the most prospective enemy. China was not involved, because China was not much then. It still isn't a great deal. Although now that it has a very limited atomic capability, it's more and more in our thinking. At that time we had a tremendous advantage in our atomic power over the Russians. We hadn't reached the point where apparently we are now--parity in certain areas. I imagine we just hope that it will be a deterrent.

Before I leave the Joint Staff, I should say that one of the things I was quite impressed with was how well the Air Force was organized to promote the Air Force concept in all the deliberations of the Joint Staff and the meetings of the Joint Chiefs. I thought that they were much better organized, in that there was never a time that the Air Force member didn't know what the party line was. I found out later that all the Air Force people would have a get-together about once a month over at Andrews Air Force Base. The operational deputies and the top people would lay out the party line so they would know what it was.

Everybody had a party line to a degree. It was Navy thinking and Army thinking and Air Force thinking. There were definite party lines, and there were a lot of conflicts of ideas. I didn't really run into it too seriously until some years later when I came in to be the director of the Strategic Plans Group. That's when the going was quite tough.

There has always been a conflict of concepts between the three armed forces--including the Marines on the Navy side--as to how the defense budget will be cut and who will get what. Of course, the basis of all of that is the force levels that are approved as part of a JCS paper. The Army will have so many divisions and certain responsibilities, the Air Force so many of this and that, and that determines how the defense money will be spent. It actually gets down to a matter of dollars and cents.

After two years on the Joint staff I was ordered to Pearl Harbor on Admiral Radford's staff.* I reported as

---

*Admiral Arthur W. Radford, USN, served as Commander in Chief Pacific/Commander in Chief U.S. Pacific Fleet, from 30 April 1949 to 10 July 1953. He was later Chairman of the Joint Chiefs of Staff.

a captain, and I was put in charge of the planning section of the Pacific Fleet. Shortly thereafter I was selected for flag rank and became a rear admiral, so I was moved out of that job. At that time Admiral Radford was Commander in Chief of the Pacific Fleet, and he was also Commander in Chief Pacific, a unified command. However, the latter was more of a facade than anything else, because neither the Army or the Air Force would participate in that command. They just wouldn't recognize that the Pacific Command was a unified joint command. Actually, most of the officers out there, including Admiral Radford, to a great extent felt that the most important command was the U.S. Pacific Fleet.

At that time Johnny Gingrich was the chief of staff of the Pacific Fleet.* I discussed this matter with him, and we both agreed that probably the thing to do was to start organizing a proper joint staff for the unified command. And if we did that, we should have at least two objectives. One was to highlight that that was a unified command staff, that it was supposed to be the overall command out there. The other was to prepare the staff and people for a time when it really would be a unified command and operate as such. We went down and discussed it with Admiral Radford. He said, "Okay, we'll make you the chief of the joint staff. You start assembling the staff." So I

---

*Rear Admiral John E. Gingrich, USN.

T. J. Hedding #2 - 170

assembled a small staff of Army, Air Force, and Navy, and we embarked upon a program.

Q: Any trouble getting personnel assigned to that staff?

Admiral Hedding: No, no trouble with the Navy, and not too much trouble with the Army and the Air Force, but they really didn't go along with it at first. As things developed, the joint unified concept became more acceptable. Just about the time that we were getting well organized, the Joint Chiefs reached a decision to take away the responsibility for Taiwan and the Philippines from General MacArthur and give it to Admiral Radford as Commander in Chief Pacific, the unified commander.

The first thing the admiral said was, "You go down and find out what it's all about." I got in a plane and took off for the Philippines. I spent considerable time with the Army command there and the 13th Air Force, which was the Air Force command at Clark Field. I discussed the shift of responsibility with the commanding general, who was an old friend of mine. I pointed out to him that under the new concept he should report to Admiral Radford as CinCPac. He said, "I can't do that. My orders are to report to Far East Command, General Weyland, who works for General MacArthur."*

---
*Lieutenant General Otto P. Weyland, USAF, Commander Far East Air Forces.

I said, "Well, that's going to be one of the problems we're going to have to straighten out, because you can't be in this area and be part of the forces assigned to the Pacific Command without reporting to the commander in chief as your superior."

We finally worked it out, but there were many troubles in getting it done. Actually, we really didn't get it solved until General MacArthur left.*

Then going into Taiwan was most interesting. That's when I first got to know the Chinese, and I think they are a very wonderful people. I know all of them from Generalissimo and Madame Chiang right on down the line.** So I made the survey and came back and reported to the admiral what I'd found.

We then set up his first visit to his new command. We went out and made the swing. We always went up to Japan, because at that time the Korean War was going on. We had to touch base with the command out there and talk to Admiral Turner Joy, who was the naval commander.*** He also had the responsibility for negotiating with the North Koreans. So we worked with his staff quite closely, because the Pacific Fleet had to furnish the naval forces

---
*MacArthur was relieved as Commander in Chief Far East Command in April 1951.
**Generalissimo Chiang Kai-shek was for many years the leader of the Nationalist Chinese government on Taiwan.
***Vice Admiral C. Turner Joy, USN, Commander Naval Forces Far East.

for that command. They actually belonged to us, and we would send them out there. We would train them and would provide logistic support for them.

When we got into Formosa, it was a very interesting aspect of the command responsibility, to work with the Chinese because we supported them completely in every way, economically and militarily. And they provided a defensive bastion for us out there, right down the chain from Japan. We were in Japan, Okinawa, and the Philippines--a natural strategic barrier against the Chinese.

Of course, the Generalissimo felt all along that his objective was to return to the mainland. I don't think we saw it quite that way; we wanted to keep him there in Taiwan. He was a most interesting person to talk to. He understood English quite well, but he wouldn't speak English. I think he was afraid he wouldn't express himself the way he wanted to. So we always had an interpreter when we talked. Of course, Madame Chiang was quite different; she spoke fluent English. They were a very charming couple. I had dinner with them many times. As a matter of fact, they kind of adopted me as one of their sons.

Q: Did you visit their home?

Admiral Hedding: Oh yes, many times. One of their homes was up on a mountain outside of Taipei, and the other one

T. J. Hedding #2 - 173

was down in the southern part of the island near Kaohsiung. When I was down there, I ran into a very interesting person, Bill Bullitt, who had been ambassador to France and Russia. He was a most interesting character.*

Q: What was he doing over there?

Admiral Hedding: Ambassador Bullitt was very anti-Communist, a very wealthy man, and he was also anti-Semitic in many ways. He used to have a vacation spot in Florida until it was more or less taken over by the Jews. Then he had a villa or something in Acapulco. Then he said he finally found a place where there wouldn't be any of them; that was in Taiwan. He said, "They can't compete with the Chinese because the Chinese to a degree are the Jews of the Orient; they're the businessmen."

Right next to the Generalissimo's beach house Ambassador Bullitt built his own little villa. He used native labor to build it and everything, but the plumbing and electrical installations he got from the United States. I visited with him several times. He was a most interesting person to talk to, very strong ideas about many things. He was violently anti-Communist. He's dead now. He had a lovely home in Washington. When I'd get back there, I'd see him there too.

---
*William C. Bullitt (1891-1967) served as U.S. ambassador to Russia, 1933-36, and to France, 1936-41. He was a special assistant to the Secretary of the Navy in 1942.

Q: That must have been quite an organizational problem--to get the first idea over to the other services that they had to comply.

Admiral Hedding: The concept of the unified command jobs was set up, and the battle had to be fought primarily in Washington. They were parceled out all over the world, and each service had a commander for it. The Army would have it here, the Air Force would have it here, and somebody else would have it there. So the concept was accepted, but in the actual implementation in the Pacific Command, the Air Force and the Army just wouldn't go about it. They finally won out. They got perhaps a little different thinking by the Chiefs of Staff and CNOs and finally worked this thing out. So the Pacific Command became established as a real unified command. Separate headquarters were set up from the Pacific Fleet headquarters, and it became the number-one command. That was actually accomplished when Admiral Stump was out there.* His deputy at that time was Admiral Curts.**

When this concept was finally approved by the other forces, Admiral Stump then relinquished his hat at

---

*Admiral Felix B. Stump, USN, held both the joint command and the Pacific Fleet command from 10 July 1953 to 14 January 1958, when he was relieved of the fleet command. He was joint Commander in Chief Pacific Commander in Chief Pacific from 14 January 1958 to 31 July of that year.
**Vice Admiral Maurice E. Curts, USN.

T. J. Hedding #2 - 175

CinCPacFlt and Admiral Curts was made CinCPacFlt. Admiral Stump moved up to the Aiea hospital installation and set up there. Air Force and Army deputies were assigned and a large joint staff headquarters set up. That's the way it operates now under Admiral McCain.*

Q: That takes you up to July '53, when you became Commander of the Formosa Patrol Force.

Admiral Hedding: Yes. I've gone through most of my time with Admiral Radford in setting up the Pacific Command joint staff and getting things organized, so when it eventually became a true unified command the staff was ready to take over the responsibilities.

Q: Would it be too much to ask you to cover just the next year, from July '53 to August '54, as Commander Formosa Patrol Force?

Admiral Hedding: When Admiral Radford was selected as Chairman of the Joint Chiefs and went back to Washington, he wanted me to come back with him. I said, "Look, Admiral, I've been working for you practically my whole career as a flag officer. How about going out and working

---

*Admiral John S. McCain, Jr., USN, served as Commander in Chief Pacific from 31 July 1968 to 1 September 1972.

at my profession as a naval officer again?"

He said, "Well, what do you want to do?"

I said, "How about the Formosa Patrol Force?"

He said, "Okay."

Q: Had that been in existence before?

Admiral Hedding: Oh, yes. A friend of mine, Binney Williamson, was commanding it.* So I got orders to command the Formosa Patrol Force. In the meantime, Admiral Stump had relieved Admiral Radford as CinCPacFlt, and I was relieved by Admiral Storrs.**

I had the Formosa Patrol Force for a year. I had two flagships, large aviation tenders. We stayed at sea the whole time. We were usually at anchor in the Pescadores, where we set up a seaplane base, or Buckner Bay in Okinawa. We had patrol planes operating from an Air Force base on Okinawa and down in the Philippines, where we operated planes out of Sangley Point. So I would just rotate from one to the other. It was just a routine year's job as Commander Formosa Patrol Force. At that time we were running reconnaissance patrols along the China coast. We were observing all the shipping and just things like that.

Q: Any crises arrive in that period?

---
*Rear Admiral Thomas Binney Williamson, USN.
**Rear Admiral Aaron P. Storrs III, USN.

Admiral Hedding: No crises; everything was very routine. I stayed there until Admiral Kivette relieved me a year later.* It was a rather trying year in that we were away from our families for a year. It became quite a problem sometimes as far as the morale of the staff to be away from their families for such a long period. In time of war you more or less expect it, but this was peacetime. To be away for one solid year was not good, so when I came back I made some strong recommendations that the policy be changed and the command be home-ported in Okinawa, which was done. Then the admiral and the staff were given quarters ashore. That took care of the problem.

Q: Did you make any new contacts or new friends with people in the Far East during that period?

Admiral Hedding: No, I was in and out of Formosa all the time, and I saw all my friends there.

Q: When was the issue of Quemoy and Matsu? That was not during that period?

Admiral Hedding: That was about that time. I don't remember whether it was when I was there or not. Matsu was

---
*Rear Admiral Frederick N. Kivette, USN.

T. J. Hedding #2 - 178

so far up north that it was very difficult for the Chinese to defend and support adequately. It took a great amount of their efforts to provide the defense for an island that wasn't particularly important. Quemoy, which is right across from the Pescadores, right near Swatow, was much more important. So we supported the Chinese in holding that, and we still support them. I think they're well dug in, and I don't think the Communists will ever dig them out. But Matsu was not worth the effort to defend it.

Q: So then in August or '54 you went back to Washington.

Admiral Hedding: Yes, I went back for my second tour on the Joint Staff.

T. J. Hedding #3 - 179

Interview Number 3 with Vice Admiral Truman J. Hedding,
U.S. Navy (Retired)

Place: Admiral Hedding's home, Coronado, California

Date: Sunday, 2 May 1971

Interviewer: Etta-Belle Kitchen

Q: I believe that the last interview terminated with your duty as Commander Formosa Patrol Force. We are now up to August 17, 1954, when you reported as Deputy Director of the Joint Strategic Plans Group in the Joint Staff office of the Joint Chiefs of Staff, Washington, D.C. To begin the background for your duty there, Admiral, would you set the stage as to who was the Chairman of the Joint Chiefs and some of the personalities in Washington at the time.

Admiral Hedding: I was detached as Commander Formosa Patrol Force in July and reported to the Joint Staff in August of '54. At that time Admiral Radford was the Chairman of the Joint Chiefs. An Army lieutenant general was the director of the Joint Staff. I relieved Admiral Cat Brown, who at that time was the Deputy Director for the Joint Strategic Plans Group.* This was my second tour of duty on the Joint Staff and with the Joint Strategic Plans Group. My background, previous duty, certainly was a help to me in carrying out my responsibilities as the director

---
*Rear Admiral Charles R. Brown, USN, later Commander Sixth Fleet during the Suez crisis of 1956.

of the strategic planning for the Joint Staff.

At this particular time there was considerable competition between the Army, Navy, and Air Force as to budget money. There was a great deal of battling back and forth and promoting of the "party line" in the planning business in supporting individual service views.

Basically, the Strategic Planning Group developed three plans for submission to the Joint Chiefs. The Joint Emergency Plan was the plan to conduct a major war with the forces in being. The Joint Strategic Objectives Plan was the plan looking five to ten years ahead, in which we tried to set forth what we would like to have in the way of forces to fight a war that might come. Then there was the long-range plan, which went well down the road to determine in general the types of weapons we would use or would like to have or what we might have in a broad picture of what a war in that time phase would be.

In addition to these three war plans, the Joint Strategic Plans Group was required, as directed by the Joint Chiefs, to prepare position papers on a great many problems faced by the Joint Chiefs. The only other planning group at that time on the Joint Staff, with the way it was organized, was the Joint Logistics Planning Group. But practically all the basic planning work was done by the Strategic Plans Group.

This group was composed of several teams. Each team was comprised of three officers from each of the services, and they were assigned specific areas of planning responsibilities. They were given color coding names to identify their areas of planning responsibility. For example, there was the White Team, which would work entirely on the Joint Emergency Plan. Another team, say, the Red Team, would be working on another plan. And the Rainbow Team would be working on all atomic energy matters. The officers assigned to the Joint Staff were usually in the captain or colonel rank, and they certainly were a very fine group of officers--most intelligent and capable.

I feel every service went out of its way to assign outstanding officers to the Joint Staff, because they recognized the importance to each service of having good basic thinking reflecting their service and their service experience. However, at that particular time there was a great deal of, let's say, infighting in order for each service to achieve what it felt it would need in order to carry out its responsibilities in the various strategic plans. The thing that affected most planning was the determination of force levels that were deemed necessary to carry out the Emergency War Plan, and also to determine the forces required in the Objectives Plan, because that in itself would determine what each service thought it should get in the way of force levels.

The force levels approved were the basic factor in determining the amount of money each service got to support those forces and equip those forces and to operate those forces. So there was a great deal of service rivalry that went into the planning. It was not so much on the Joint Staff that this occurred, because my experience on both tours of duty was that the Joint Staff Planning Groups arrived at very objective and reasonable solutions to planning problems or any problems assigned to them.

The way the system worked was that the output of the Joint Staff would be turned over for approval by the Joint Strategic Plans Committee prior to submission to the Joint Chiefs. That committee consisted of a chairman, the director of the Strategic Planning Group, and the planning representative of each of the three services, plus a Marine planner whenever any of these subjects under consideration was of interest to the Marine Corps.

It was in this particular area, the deliberations of the planning committee, that the so-called party lines made it most difficult to arrive at reasonable solutions or reasonable compromises. It was not at the working level where the difficulty came, where the plans were prepared by the Joint Staff. It was in the planning committee, which consisted of the planners of each of the three services. They were not members of the Joint Staff, other than being members of this committee. They were actually assigned to duty as directors of strategic planning in each of the service staffs.

We usually met two or three times a week to consider position papers or plans. Once the Strategic Plans Committee would approve a paper, it would then go on up to the Joint Chiefs for final approval. However, with most of the controversial subjects we never arrived at an agreed solution. They were most always split. Sometimes they would be split three ways; there'd be an Army position, a Navy position, and an Air Force position.

It was very frustrating for me to try to get the services to reach a reasonable compromise or a reasonable solution, rather than forwarding "split" papers up to the Chiefs. I felt that a great many of these could be decided at the committee level.

Q: If there were three positions, it seems as though they hardly needed them.

Admiral Hedding: That was the point. In retrospect, it was the reason why within a year or two the Chairman of the Joint Chiefs disestablished this committee. I pointed out to them time after time, "If you don't reach a solution on this, you're failing to meet your responsibilities. You're merely passing the buck on up to the Joint Chiefs." They still would do it. So, as I mentioned, within a year or

T. J. Hedding #3 - 184

two the Joint Strategic Plans Committee was disestablished; it was just thrown out. The papers, which were usually very good papers, would go directly up to the Chiefs.

I realize that at times there were certain basic conflicts of principles or ideas that the committee would have to submit as a split paper to the Chiefs. But most of the time the solutions were real good papers. They were joint and reflected as far as possible the views and experience of all three services in the group from the Joint Staff. But they would get into the committee, and the committee would just tear them apart.

I talked to each of the service planners individually to try to get them to see if they couldn't in most cases reach reasonable solutions, but it seemed to be an impossible task at that time.

Q: They weren't very useful.

Admiral Hedding: They could have been, because they could have done a lot of the basic homework for the Joint Chiefs and for the operational deputies. I know Admiral Radford used to call me in many times and ask what was the trouble. I would sit in when we would brief the admiral on the papers that were going to appear before the Joint Chiefs. The team that prepared the paper would come into the admiral's office and would brief him on the paper, the

T. J. Hedding #3 - 185

plan, or whatever it was, and he would ask questions. He was always impressed by what a good solution the Joint Staff had made, but by the time it got to the Chiefs--when the committee got through with it--it had no resemblance many times to the paper that we had prepared. So it was rather, in a way, a frustrating business.

Q: Was the bad feeling that had been engendered in the previous decade still being reflected among the various services?

Admiral Hedding: I wouldn't call it so much of a bad feeling as it was service rivalry to obtain funds, to obtain money, because each service, I think, honestly felt that it needed so much. They needed certain forces to carry out their responsibilities within the plans. That's where the basic rivalry was, although it did spill over many times into just party line. I wouldn't point the finger at any one service as being too much influenced by the party line; I think all of them were in certain areas.

Q: Do you have any example that you can recall?

Admiral Hedding: No, not particularly, because when you look back on those things now, they sometimes seem rather childish. But they were indicative of the period at that time when there was considerable rivalry between the three services and, as we used to call, "the promoting of the party line." A lot of their thinking was rather parochial in that they would lose the broad concept and the main objective in trying to promote the party line.

Q: I was wondering if you could give an example to show the type of thing you're describing.

Admiral Hedding: I don't think you need to have any specific example. It's just that the basic objective of each service is to get as much of the defense appropriations that it felt it needed. The Navy wanted to maintain as many carriers as they could with the forces afloat. The Air Force wanted as many air wings. The Army wanted as many divisions and all the supporting activities. Normally, when you added up what they all said they needed, the bill was too high. There just wasn't that kind of money available. So they'd each have to pare down their requirements, and that's where the infighting came up. The Navy said it had to have so many ships, and the Air Force had to carry out the job set forth in its plans, and so many of this and so many of that. Any time anything affected the force levels or the funding for the services, there was always a conflict.

Q: I'm sure it would have been difficult for any one service to say, "Well, we can get along with less."

Admiral Hedding: They couldn't very well, because if they did, they were just in trouble. So it finally went up to the Joint Chiefs for them to decide. Sometimes when the Chiefs themselves couldn't decide, the Secretary of Defense would decide it. There was many a battle, let's call it, or conflicts of ideas between the Joint Chiefs themselves.

I know Admiral Radford used to tell them, "Look, you're professional officers. You have to decide these things. If you don't decide and we send a split paper up to the Secretary of Defense, the decision is going to be made by civilians. So you'd better get yourselves together and make a decision that has to be made based on military thinking and military experience. Otherwise, you may not like what finally comes out of the Secretary of Defense's office where the decision will be made. It will be made by the Secretary of Defense and his civilian assistants." I think they appreciated that thought.

I was on the Joint Strategic Plans Group for just about a year, until May 1955, when I was relieved.

Q: Before we get to that, do you recall the need of a split paper going to the Secretary of Defense, or were they eventually able to be resolved at the JCS level?

Admiral Hedding: Most of them were resolved at the JCS level, but there were some where the splits were so basic that they were sent up to the Secretary of Defense for decision.

Q: Do you recall any of those?

Admiral Hedding: No, I don't recall any, but most of them had to do with the basic strategic plans and the basic force levels. That was the keystone of all planning--force levels. That was where the basic conflicts were--to determine the force levels.

Q: You started to say who relieved you in that job.

Admiral Hedding: I was relieved by an Air Force major general. I don't recall his name, as a matter of fact. Then I reported as a special assistant to the Chairman of the Joint Chiefs of Staff, Admiral Radford, relieving Rear Admiral George Anderson.*

Q: How did your duties change?

---

*Rear Admiral George W. Anderson, USN, later became a four-star admiral and served as Chief of Naval Operations from 1961 to 1963. His two-volume oral history is in the Naval Institute collection.

Admiral Hedding: They changed considerably in that I was primarily the senior assistant to the chairman. The title was Special Assistant to the Chairman. I was there for about a year. That was a very interesting time. I had worked for Admiral Radford so often, and had been with him so often, that it was very natural. It was a very easy thing for me to slide into this job, also having had previous experience on the Joint Staff.

I was his assistant. Everything that went to him I saw before it got to him, except perhaps some personal things. He had a small staff. He had two aides--a young Air Force lieutenant colonel, a young Marine lieutenant colonel, and some other assistants. He had one Air Force colonel, who had been with us on the joint staff out in Pearl Harbor, who more or less was in charge of everything that went on his desk. He was in the outer office. And he also had a congressional liaison officer. We had an Army colonel who was assigned many jobs, but his main job was to prepare speeches for the admiral. Then we had a group of three officers, one from each service, who were the Chairman's Special Study Group. We would assign them papers to be looked over and briefs to be prepared on them for the Chairman.

He, as Chairman, had many responsibilities. He saw many people. He appeared before the Congress with the

Secretary of Defense to testify. Of course, he had access with the Secretary of Defense to the President and Vice President.

Q: Did you go with him on those?

Admiral Hedding: No. Normally when he appeared before the congressional committees to testify with the Secretary of Defense, the congressional liaison officer, a Navy captain, would go along with him.

Whenever he had any callers or appointments with any foreigners or anyone other than a friendly one--more or less a social one--I always would be in his office. I think he did that for two reasons--so that he could have someone there to report on what the discussions were and what was said and to write them up. After each of these appointments I would write up what was discussed and what was said by both by the admiral and whoever was calling, so that would be a matter of record. So he could always refer to, "When So-and-so called, we discussed so-and-so, and this and that were said."

During this time the service rivalry in the party line really became at times quite violent, you might say. I think at this time this led up to his pointing out to the Chiefs personally that in a lot of these things they should take the recommendations of the Joint Staff rather than

T. J. Hedding #3 - 191

passing the papers up to the Secretary of Defense. I think it was during this time that the Chairman, Admiral Radford, decided to do away with the Joint Strategic Plans Committee, because rather than assisting the Joint Chiefs at arriving at proper solutions, they were hindering them by sending so many split papers up.

Q: You pointed out the other assistants that Admiral Radford had. What is the meaning of the title special assistant?

Admiral Hedding: I was the senior assistant; I was a flag officer. You might say I was the executive officer in his office.

The Joint Staff came under the Chairman, but the day-to-day workings of the Joint Staff were under the director of the Joint Staff, who was a three-star general or flag officer. Then, of course, under the director were the Joint Strategic Plans, the Joint Logistics, the Joint Intelligence, and other special groups. They all came under the Chairman, because he headed up the Joint Staff. Of course, you might say he had two hats. He was a member of the corporate body, heading up the Joint Chiefs of Staff, and he also headed up the Joint Staff.

It was amazing to me how the office of the Secretary of Defense and the Joint Staff and the whole business down in the Defense Department grew from the original concept. I think the original concept was that the Secretary of Defense would have a relatively small staff. I believe the Joint Staff was originally limited by law to not over 200. It's grown now. There are literally thousands in the Defense Department, and the Joint Staff has grown and expanded to I don't know what size.

They later put the Joint Staff in operations of the services that they didn't have when I was there. There's now a Joint Operations Group on the Joint Staff that is responsible for the operations of the armed forces. In other words, the way it used to be, the chief of each service was responsible, as a member of the Joint Chiefs, for the operations of his service, and he had his own operations groups. But now the operations of the unified commands, which actually comprise all those armed forces that are deployed worldwide, are run by the Joint Chiefs of Staff as a corporate group under the Secretary of Defense and the President. There is a Joint Operations Group on the Joint Staff, but it wasn't there when I was there.

Q: You compare your job as special assistant to executive officer.

Admiral Hedding: Yes, that would be as good a description as anything.

Q: You must have seen lots of important decisions made in this year.

Admiral Hedding: There were. I don't remember exactly what they were, but there were always things coming up. When you have an outfit as big as the Defense Department, there are important decisions being made all the time.

Q: Do you remember some of the important problems that developed in this year?

Admiral Hedding: The important problems, again, came down to the two joint planning documents--the Joint Strategic Emergency Plan and the Joint Strategic Objectives Plan. They would have to be decided every year as approved plans so that there would be a war plan that could be executed and implemented in case we did go to war. At that particular time the war would be a war with Russia. There were other local plans, contingency plans, plans for things like Korea.

Q: Korea had wound down by this time. Were there plans related to anything comparable to our Vietnamese involvement?

Admiral Hedding: At that particular time decisions had to be made as to what we would do in Southeast Asia. We entered into several treaties there. We had a treaty with Australia and New Zealand and Great Britain. SEATO was the Southeast Asia treaty.* We had a number of these groups in Southeast Asia where we set up commitments.

Q: And the Geneva Convention had been in 1954.

Admiral Hedding: The Geneva Convention was a convention covering conflicts. Within the Geneva Convention is the treatment of prisoners of war, which North Vietnam and South Vietnam were parties to.

Q: I wondered if there was anything at that time, in looking back, you could forecast . . . ?

Admiral Hedding: No, because those things were quite a few years ago. I kept no diaries or anything, and it's hard to remember other than just an overall impression of what went on during that period. The major impression at this particular time was the continual trouble we were having in planning, due to the so-called party lines and service conflicts as to what should be or should not be done.

I was detached in June 1956 and reported as Commander

---
*SEATO--Southeast Asia Treaty Organization.

T. J. Hedding #3 - 195

Carrier Division Three. I also deployed as Commander Task Force 77, the carriers deployed in the Western Pacific. I reported on 13 September 1956 as Commander Carrier Division Three. I was there for about a year. I was deployed about half the time in the Western Pacific. At that particular time there was no real active combat, and it was more or less a routine tour.

At that time I had already made up my mind that I was going to retire, and it was just a question of going about it. I had made up my mind one time before and wanted to retire before I reached the statutory age limit. I just was not interested in fighting my way up the three- and four-star ladder. I'd seen too much of the infighting and things that went on, and in a way it disgusted me a little bit. The three- and four-star jobs are mostly political-- not all of them but most of them. There were certain senior flag officers on active duty that had considerable influence on who was selected for the three- and four-star assignments. If you weren't on somebody's team, supposedly your chances were slim.

I had decided that I would retire from the Navy. When my year out in the Pacific was through, I requested and was assigned to duty as the Bureau of Aeronautics general representative of the western district. This assignment is normally made to an aeronautical engineering duty only officer. However, since I had an aeronautical engineering degree, I was qualified. And since I had asked for it, I got the job. I relieved Admiral Pearson, who was an AEDO. He retired and went with North American Aviation.*

I had this job for two years. I asked for it with the idea of making contacts in the defense industries so that when I did retire, I'd retire to a good job in the defense industry. I wanted to do this reasonably early so that I would still have productive years ahead of me.

I did retire in '59, at which time I was 57 years old. I would have had five more years in the Navy if I had stayed on. However, I had made up my mind. So those last two years I was the bureau representative with my headquarters in Los Angeles. The reason I selected that was because a great deal of the defense business is located on the West Coast. I spent those last two years going around to practically all the defense industries in the country, not just on the West Coast. I started with Boeing and went to everything on the West Coast. I went East and to every place that I felt I wanted to learn something about the defense industry and what they were doing.

Of course, in my job I had entree to any place I wanted to go, which made it very fine. I got to meet the top people and through them their chief engineers. I got to go through their plants and see what they were doing and discuss what they were doing. It was a very educational

---
*Rear Admiral John B. Pearson, USN.

T. J. Hedding #3 - 197

period for me. I learned a lot about the defense industry. That was about the middle of 1958 when I just about decided that now was the time. It was known in the industry that I was going to retire, and I had two or three very nice offers from the defense industry.

About that time the general manager of the Delco-Remy division of General Motors, Mr. Don Boyes, came out to the West Coast. He came out there to learn something about the defense industry, because, as I said, the West Coast is one of the major centers of the defense industry. Through one of the General Motors local representatives an appointment was made, and he came to my office one morning and introduced himself. He had his chief engineer and another one of his staff with him. He said what they were there for. I said, "Let's sit down and talk about it." So we discussed the defense industry, and I asked questions about what Delco-Remy did and why they were interested in it.

I told him, "If you're interested in getting into the defense business to make money, and I understand that General Motors likes to make money, this is not the business to be in. But there are several sound reasons, if you're really interested in it, how you could get something out of being in the defense business. The Department of Defense, through the three services, is engaged in many highly technical programs and very expensive programs that only the Defense Department could afford to engage in. And by participating in some of these far-out programs, you might learn something that would be of interest and provide some technical fallout in your business. That would be really your main objective, as I see it, for getting in this--to get technical fallout. The way you learn about these things is not by reading about them but by having your people participate in them, because your knowledge is in the brains of your people and not in your plants or anything else. So if you want to learn something about it, you have to participate; you can't get it by reading it."

He said, "That makes sense."

I said, "There's another reason; I think it's a rather intangible one. I feel, from my point of view, that General Motors should participate in the defense business because they have a great deal to contribute in the way of knowledge and experience. And I think probably a third reason would be in the event we ever face another national emergency and General Motors would be required to stop building automobiles and start building airplanes and tanks and military products, you need some people in your organization who are familiar with defense activities."

He said, "That also makes a lot of sense."

I said, "There's going to be a three- or four-day meeting in St. Louis at the McDonnell Aircraft Company, at which representatives from all the defense industries will be there. There will be papers read, there will be

T. J. Hedding #3 - 199

symposiums, and quite an exchange of information. I think it might be very worthwhile for you and your chief engineer and anyone else of your division to attend. If you're interested, I will arrange," which I did.

About two weeks before the meeting, I got a call from Mr. Boyes saying he had a couple more people who would like to come. Could I arrange for them to come? Then I saw them in St. Louis and spent some time with Mr. Boyes and his boss, Mr. Skinner, discussing the problem of Delco-Remy getting into the defense business.

I suggested, "What you need on your staff, and I'm sure you don't have anyone perhaps as knowledgeable as they should be, is someone really knowledgeable in the defense business. He can advise you as to what areas would be worthwhile for you to attempt to get into and those that wouldn't be worthwhile. I think the best way to get this knowledge is to get some retired Navy or Air Force officer who has been in the defense business and hire him as an assistant."

He said, "That makes sense." They had several discussions, and they approached me and said, "How about you?"

I said, "Well, I hadn't thought about getting in General Motors. I have certainly considered and plan to retire and get in the defense business, but we might discuss it."

He said, "Suppose you fly on up to Anderson, Indiana, instead of flying directly back to Los Angeles? I have my own plane, crew, pilot, and everything."

I said, "Sure, I think it would be a good idea."

"Suppose you get in my plane and we'll fly up."

So we flew up and landed at Anderson. I spent a couple of days there going all through the Delco-Remy plants, seeing what they were doing, what they were interested in, and their research group. I was quite impressed with it. I said, "I'll consider it." When I got back, I wrote and said, "I'd like to very much." One thing led to another, and I requested retirement. I retired on January 1, 1959 and went to work for Don Boyes in the Delco-Remy Division of General Motors.

They said, "Where do you want to make your headquarters?"

I said, "Certainly it won't be in Anderson, because I don't think that Anderson is one of the centers of the defense industry. I think Los Angeles is one of the centers of the defense industry. I think Los Angeles is probably one of the best places where I can keep current and have knowledge of what's going on, and I have many contacts in that area. I think it would be best for me to set up my shop in the Los Angeles area."

He said, "I think that's a good idea."

I first had an office in the battery plant at Anaheim,

but that was too far from where I lived, so I suggested I get another office. Then I got another office in Beverly Hills. About the first six months were more or less a getting-acquainted period for me to learn more about Delco-Remy and General Motors. The job that I had, being assistant to the general manager, certainly gave me entree to everything in General Motors. He took me up to Detroit, where I met everyone in the executive group of General Motors. The president was Mr. John Gordon, a Naval Academy graduate, class of '22, who had been at the Naval Academy at the same time I was. I had a nice visit with him and the senior vice president, Mr. Roger Keyes, whom I met when he came in as Deputy Secretary of Defense with Mr. Wilson.* Mr. Wilson brought him in for a year, and then he went back to General Motors, so I had known him. I met all the top people in General Motors.

I spent some time with Larry Hafstad, who was a vice president of General Motors and ran the General Motors research in Detroit.** He had worked with the Navy. I got to know him and went through their research and what they were doing. So at the end of what we call in the Navy the "make-you-learn" period, we started getting down to what areas would be worthwhile for Delco-Remy.

---

*Charles E. Wilson served as Secretary of Defense from 28 January 1953 to 8 October 1957 under President Dwight D. Eisenhower.
**Lawrence R. Hafstad was a vice president for General Motors and director of the research laboratories from 1955 to 1969. In 1946 the Secretary of the Navy awarded him a medal of merit for World War II ordnance developments.

We had a very good group of electrical chemists in the battery department, so we decided that we would be in the business of the silver-zinc battery. The silver-zinc battery is a very exotic type of battery. The active elements in the battery are silver and zinc with a potassium hydroxide electrolyte. It is what is called a primary battery. You introduce the electrolyte into the cells, and immediately it's almost an electrical explosion. You get a very high output. It's used in missiles. It was used in the atomic bomb, because within a fraction of a second to initiate the explosion, the first thing you do when the bomb takes off or the missile takes off, you charge the batteries by forcing the electrolyte into the cells. So you immediately have a high electrical output that runs everything in the missile--all the guidance systems. It's a very exotic battery, and there weren't too many companies in that business. The batteries were very expensive. They would run somewhere around $2,000 apiece for, say, the Minuteman missile.*

It was the Minuteman missile that I got interested in, because they were just at the stage where North American was developing the guidance system, and that was quite a big problem. So I said, "I think maybe that's where we should go. I think we've something that maybe we can sell." I arranged to meet with the people at North

---
*The Minuteman was a land-based intercontinental ballistic missile capable of delivering a nuclear warhead.

American Electronics in Downey. We discussed it with them. They were interested, like anybody would be, in a General Motors division, so we worked with them.

They said, "Have you got a battery?"

I said, "No, we haven't got a battery. We'll see if we can build one that can meet your requirements and specifications."

So they gave us the specifications and said, "How much will it cost?"

I talked this over with Mr. Boyes. I said, "What we would like to do is to build two or three batteries at our expense to see whether we can come anywhere near meeting your requirements and specifications. Then we can sit down and maybe we can do business that way." So that's what we did. We were successful, and we developed the battery. All the batteries in the Minuteman missile are made by Delco-Remy, and they've been very successful.

There were other areas, and there were lots of things they thought they might want to get into. I probably did as much recommending not to get into this as I did to get into it. It was a very rewarding experience to me to work for Delco-Remy at General Motors, particularly in the position that I had.

I attended two of their management conferences down at Greenbrier. About every three years they'd get all the top executives and go down to Greenbrier for about four days, and we'd take over Greenbrier. We'd spend the mornings listening to presentations by the top people in General Motors. In the afternoons you were free and could play golf or fish or trapshoot or what have you. Then we'd usually have a cocktail party and a dinner party, and they'd bring a show down from Broadway. It gives you an opportunity to meet the top people on a social basis, which is quite important.

The first time I was down there, there were about 750 executives from General Motors from all over the world, their top people. They had a group of tables, and each table would seat about 20 people. At the end of each table they had a little placard, which would give the name of a senior executive, perhaps one of the board of directors or the president or one of the vice presidents or general managers, who would be at that table. So I would go in and look around and find somebody at a table that I didn't know that I wanted to meet. Then I would go to that table and sit down by this person for dinner. That way I got to meet some very interesting people.

One time I went in there, and I sat next to Mr. Alfred P. Sloan, who was "Mr. General Motors."* He didn't know me, so I introduced myself and told him who I was. He was most interested in what I was doing. Those four days were

---
*Sloan (1875-1966) had served as both president and chairman of the board of directors of General Motors.

just wonderful. You'd get to meet people like that.

During this period I maintained my contacts with the Defense Department, a lot of times going around to various meetings and seeing people and being seen, which is part of the job. It was very, very worthwhile, and I enjoyed it thoroughly.

Q: How long did you stay with General Motors?

Admiral Hedding: I stayed with General Motors until 1965. I got out then because my wife was ill with cancer. I felt that I couldn't devote time to her and also time to my job. So I spoke with Mr. Boyes and told him that I thought it best that I retire, which I did. I retired from General Motors in 1965.

During the period I was there, it was a most rewarding experience. General Motors is a very large organization, and like big organizations they have the same problems that a big organization like the Navy has, and General Motors is comparable in size. They had at that time between 650,000 and 700,000 employees. One of the major problems, of course, is in communication, as it is in the Navy.

Another problem with an organization that big is to ensure that they get the right man at the right spot at the right time--the same thing as in the Navy. In other words, we hope that the proper people will be selected for captain and flag rank, so there is a continual screening of management types in big corporations to make sure that they receive the proper training if they're on the way up the executive ladder. And they have, in effect, the same thing that we have in the service--the fitness report system. It is very similar to the Navy's system. They try to select and evaluate talented executives, the younger men, and move them up and watch them and give them important jobs.

As a comment on that, when Admiral Burke was selected as CNO, he had two or three months before he would relieve Admiral Carney.* During that time, he thought he would go around to the big corporations and see what he could learn from them in what we call career management. So he went to Detroit and spent some time with Mr. Louis Seaton, who was the vice president for personnel at General Motors.

He was questioning him about career management, and Mr. Seaton said, "Admiral, we realize that's a very important aspect of running a big corporation, as I'm sure it is in the Navy. We have an evaluation system. The Navy calls it the fitness report, the Army calls it something else, and the Air Force calls it something else. But it is basically a system for evaluating your management talent. We were interested in how the services did it, so we sent people to interview people in each service, and we found

---
*Admiral Arleigh A. Burke, USN, relieved Admiral Robert B. Carney, USN, as Chief of Naval Operations 17 August 1955.

out that the best system we could find was the Navy system. Now here you are trying to find out from us." It was a rather interesting aside.

One of the things that impressed me most about General Motors was the tremendous amount of management talent they had and how they developed it and nurtured it. As an example, their Buick division had not been too successful for a few years, and they decided they needed some new management. So they selected a man to head up the Buick division as general manager and told him he could go out into the corporation to pick the key people he felt he'd need to help him bring this division back, so he did.

I know he came to Delco-Remy and took our production manager and took him up to Buick and made him production manager there. Then he went someplace else for a new sales manager, and someplace else for a new director of quality control, and someplace else for a new chief engineer. The thing that impressed me first was that there were people available in the corporation, and secondly that when they took them from a division, they didn't hurt that division, because there was someone that the division had already trained that could move into that position.

Another thing--I didn't find any so-called company politics or political cliques in the corporation. I'm sure there were in some of the divisions, but I know there weren't in Delco-Remy, and I didn't run it. Surely there were ambitious people in the management chain. I think practically everyone from lower management on up hoped that one day maybe he would be president of General Motors, just as in the Navy every officer has an ambition some day that he will be CNO. It really was a very worthwhile and very rewarding experience to work with a big corporation like General Motors, and I made many, many friends, and I see them frequently.

I was very fortunate--much more fortunate, I think--to work for General Motors than I would have been if I had gone to, say, one of the large defense companies here on the West Coast. Because there are many retired service people in the defense industry on the West Coast, but very few in General Motors. I think I was the only flag officer or general officer who was employed by General Motors at that time.

I know that there was quite a bit of congressional interest in all the retired service people working in the defense industry. My name was in the Congressional Record as being one of the senior people working there for General Motors, listing my salary and all this business which they did. We were all very careful that there was no conflict of interest, because we knew we couldn't get in sales. But, again, that is a very abstract business. When you work for any outfit, you're selling your outfit. You sell their capabilities. You don't go around with an order book under your arm, but you are selling something.

Just like I sold first the idea of getting into the silver-zinc business and had a major part in their contract with North American to build the silver-zinc battery for the Minuteman missile. I followed that up, and we got a contract with Hughes Aircraft for the silver-zinc battery for a missile they were building for the Navy. We had quite a few contracts.

I found something that was rather disheartening in a way. I couldn't get too much interest from a great many of the senior people, the management people in Delco-Remy, to become interested in the defense business. After I'd been there for some time, one of the management group said to me, "Truman, you don't realize it, but you came to this job with two strikes against you."

I said, "What do you mean?"

He said, "Basically, we really didn't need or want defense business. We recognize that maybe there will be some technical fallout, but we certainly also realize, and it's most important, that we're not going to make a profit and get the return on the investment in the defense business as we get in the automotive business. What we are doing when we get into the defense business is that the division will not make the profits that they'd make if they used these same talents in developing, say, a better battery for the automobile than developing a battery for a missile."

In General Motors bonus rewards are a very big thing. Your bonus at General Motors is the objective that everybody works for, because you get a very big bonus. Your bonus is determined first of all by the profits or the earnings that the corporation makes. Then that in turn filters down to how well a division does in contributing to the earnings of the corporation; then a certain amount of bonus money is assigned to this division. The general manager determines how much key people get in the way of a bonus. So most everything you do, to a degree, is oriented towards your bonus. It isn't everything, but it has a very strong impact on what you do.

For that reason, a great many of them are reluctant to engage in the defense business. Even when they were successful in the silver-zinc battery and getting this contract, they still didn't think too much of it. Because in order to develop the silver-zinc battery to be competitive and to get this contract, they had to take engineers away from working on the lead-acid battery to work on the silver-zinc battery. That cut down technical advances because you were taking your brains, your experience, away from the lead-acid battery and putting it there where you didn't get the profits. When you cut down on the profits, you cut down on the bonus.

Actually, one of the recommendations that I made to the general manager, "You restrict your defense business to not more than 5% to 10% of your total volume of business, because when you do that the effect on your earnings will be rather insignificant." The fact is that you don't make the percentage profits or the return on investment which you make in the automotive business. I pointed out at that stage that the profits in the defense business after taxes were less than 3%, so that doesn't look very good, as compared to what they get for building starters and batteries and all the other things they build.

Q: I don't know whether you are aware of it, but your enthusiasm in describing your experiences with General Motors is greater than your enthusiasm in describing some of your Navy duty. Now, is that because it's more recent?

Admiral Hedding: It's probably because it's more recent.

Looking back on my naval experience, I don't think I had anything any more rewarding to me personally than my experiences in the Navy. I was very fortunate in that I was a professional officer; I was a naval aviator; and I participated in some of the best areas that I could have participated in during World War II. In other words, I was able to put to use and do the things that I was trained to do, and I was in positions where my knowledge could be used. I was very fortunate in the jobs that I had in the Navy. The Navy was very fine to me, and I worked my tail off for the Navy.

I am also very enthusiastic about General Motors. You'd expect me to be enthusiastic about the Navy, which I am, but I just wanted to make the comparison of what I felt was how fortunate I was to have made the decision to go with General Motors rather than some defense activity.

The defense business to me is very frustrating; it's feast or famine. At one time they've got more work to do than they have people to do it. They get several contracts and they feast. Then suddenly some other outfit gets a big contract--there are not too many big contracts to go around--and they will find famine and they'll have to get rid of very important key people.

Q: Tell me what you're doing since you retired from General Motors.

Admiral Hedding: Very little. I retired in '65, and my wife died in '67. I spent those last two years helping to take care of her. When she died, I didn't know what to do. I play golf, have a lot of friends, and take life easy.

I think I'm fortunate that I had this transition period from my very active duty in the Navy to those six and a half years with General Motors, where I was in a position as an adviser or consultant rather than as an executive position. All I was doing was advising rather than making decisions. So that was a good transition period, because most of us reach a point sometime when we just stop working. Of course, some people work until they die. A lot of them work so hard that they don't live long.

I'm very happy with what I'm doing now, and that's doing practically nothing. I read a lot, play golf, and I travel. I have many friends that I discuss things with. I play bridge. It's diversion. The thing is to keep your mind working. When you have no more interests, you might as well turn in your suit.

Q: How would you describe yourself as a person? How would you describe your own personality? What kind of a person do you see yourself?

Admiral Hedding: I think I'm, you might say, a rather convivial person. I make friends easily, and I have many friends. I have a lot of friends, and I keep active. I keep active mentally and physically. I think you have to do that; without it what do you have?

Q: What do you think has been your greatest contribution in your career?

Admiral Hedding: The greatest contribution I made, I think, was my knowledge of naval aviation and my background of training and the people I was fortunate to work with. I worked with and under as bosses the leaders of naval aviation. Just name them, I worked for them: Admiral Towers, Admiral King, Admiral Sherman, Admiral Mitscher, Admiral Nimitz, Admiral Radford. I worked for all of them. You can't work for those people without learning something.

Of course, I had a very good background. Practically all my career was in carriers, so I knew carriers, as a carrier pilot or on the carriers. I think that's the major contribution I made--from my background of training and experience. I was very knowledgeable on carriers. When I worked on the Joint Staff, I learned to work with the other services. I had three jobs on the Joint Staff. I think that was a major contribution.

Q: Do you think of yourself as having any weaknesses?

Admiral Hedding: That's hard to say. I guess we all have weaknesses. I know I get along with people. I've always been able to get along with both my seniors and my juniors. A lot of naval officers or people in management get along fine in that they more or less make their main objective getting along with their seniors. I think it's equally important or sometimes more important to get along with your juniors, so you get people that are loyal to you who'll work for you.

I may be a little demanding sometimes, maybe more than I should of people. I try to demand a lot of myself. Sometimes, again, I may be a little too easygoing. It's hard to say where you do best. There're some people who are drivers and some people who are leaders. Sometimes you perhaps need both. I consider myself more of a leader than a driver. I also feel that I have a very good mind for analyzing things. I've always been able to analyze--get to the meat of the matter. I think that's probably been one of my strengths and has influenced the contributions that I have made in the Navy.

Q: Do you have any final comments that you would like to make to your biography?

Admiral Hedding: Not that I can think of. I might have some after I've read it over. That would give me a better idea perhaps.

I look back on my career in the Navy with a great deal of pride, a great deal of satisfaction. I was very fortunate in my career in that I was assigned to many positions as I moved along in increased rank that were good positions, good for me and hard-working positions. I think there are some officers who try to avoid tough jobs, or jobs too demanding, or jobs where they are afraid they will make mistakes. I've known quite a few of them. I tried never to do that. I've taken a lot of hard jobs and worked hard at them. So I look back with a great deal of satisfaction on my career in the Navy. I was very fortunate in the assignments that I got and the people that I worked for--the fact that I was on the Joint Staff, the fact that I was on the Strategic Bombing Survey, where I learned a lot of things, and things like that.

Q: It's been interesting. When you get the manuscript back, if you want to make any additions or deletions, feel free to do it.

Admiral Hedding: Do you think that I've given you everything that I could? I'm sorry that I don't have any papers or any diary to refer to.

Q: I think one's biography usually reflects the person, and I think you have described your career as you remember and saw it to be. The Institute thanks you.

Index

to

The Reminiscences of

Vice Admiral Truman J. Hedding,
United States Navy (Retired)

Aircraft Carriers
   Development of tactical doctrine in 1943 for the fast carrier task force, 37-40

   See also Carrier Division Three, Task Force 58

Air Force, U.S.
   Air Force members of the Joint Staff were well organized during the 1949-51 period in terms of the service's party line on various issues, 167-168; some of its responsibilities moved under the Pacific Command when that command became truly joint in the early 1950s, 169-172

Alcohol
   Cheap whiskey was available at the naval officers' club on Guam in the summer of 1945, 128-129

Ancon, USS (AGC-4)
   Amphibious command ship that served as a floating hotel in Tokyo for the staff of the U.S. Strategic Bombing Survey in late 1945, 131-132; Japanese Navy wartime action reports that had been stored in caves were taken aboard the ship in late 1945 to be microfilmed, 139-140. site of 1945 interview of Prince Konoye, former Japanese Prime Minister, 141-142; returned to the United States at the end of 1945, 152-153

Anderson, Major General Orvil A., USA
   Army Air Forces officer who made inflated claims concerning the effectiveness of his service's bombing campaigns in World War II, 145; role in interrogating Japanese as part of the U.S. Strategic Bombing Survey in 1945, 146-147

Antiair Warfare
   Effective U.S. antiaircraft fire during a carrier strike against the Marianas Islands in February 1944, 53

Army, U.S.
   Some of its responsibilities moved under the Pacific Command when that command became truly joint in the early 1950s, 169-172

Army Air Forces, U.S.
   Flew fighter and bomber missions from Iwo Jima after the island's capture in early 1945, 93-94; B-29 raids against Japan in the spring and summer of 1945, 120-121; in 1945 Major General Curtis LeMay declined to run bombing campaigns against Japan in coordination with Navy carrier planes, 121-123; evaluation of the role of conventional and atomic bombs in the campaign against Japan, 132-133, 138, 145; made inflated claims on behalf of its bombing effectiveness in World War II, 145-147

Atomic Bombs
See Nuclear Weapons

Averill, Commander James Kent, USN (USNA, 1927)
Killed in a plane crash in March 1944 when catapulted from a carrier, 67

Aviation Pilots
Cream-of-the-crop enlisted pilots flew as wingmen to the officers in Fighting Squadron Two in the late 1930s, 26-27

B-29 Superfortress
U.S. Army Air Forces bomber used for raids against Japan in the spring and summer of 1945, 120-121; in 1945 Major General Curtis LeMay declined to run bombing campaigns against Japan in coordination with Navy carrier planes, 121-123; evaluation of the role of atomic bombs in the campaign against Japan, 132-133

Baka Bombs
Relatively ineffectual suicide weapons employed by the Japanese in the closing stages of World War II, 154

Batteries
Electrical storage batteries manufactured in the 1950s and 1960s for use in various U.S. weapons, 202-203, 209-210

Betty
Japanese bomber based at Kwajalein that attacked U.S. carrier forces in December 1943, 49-50; based in the Marshall Islands during U.S. raid in February 1944, 53

Bombing
Major General Curtis E. LeMay of the Army Air Forces directed the tactics used in B-29 bombing raids against Japan in the spring and summer of 1945, 120-121; evaluation of the role of both conventional and atomic bombs in the campaign against Japan, 132-133, 138, 144-145; the Army Air Forces made inflated claims on behalf of its bombing effectiveness in World War II, 145-147

Boyes, Don
Delco-Remy general manager whose company was interested in the late 1950s in doing business with the Department of Defense, 197-200, 203

Bullitt, William C.
Anti-Semitic, anti-Communist individual who served as U.S. ambassador to Taiwan in the early 1950s, 173

Burke, Admiral Arleigh A., USN (USNA, 1923)
Became chief of staff to Vice Admiral Marc Mitscher in the spring of 1944, although Mitscher was initially reluctant to have him, 63-67, 83-86; airplane ride off a

carrier to become familiar with operations, 72-73; aggressive efforts in trying to get the carriers more involved during the invasion of the Marianas in June 1944, 75-78; spent time in 1955 examining promotion systems of various U.S. civilian corporations, 206-207

Carrier Division Three
Administrative organization for carriers involved in strikes against Wake and Marcus islands in late 1943, 41-42; Rear Admiral Charles Pownall was relieved as commander of the fast carrier task force in late 1943 because of a perception that he wasn't aggressive enough, 50-52; Rear Admiral Marc Mitscher became the new commander in January 1944, 52

See also Task Force 58

Chesapeake Bay
Inadequate as a training site for the carrier Essex (CV-9) in 1943, 35

Chiang Kai-shek
As leader of the Chinese nationalists in the early 1950s, Chiang nurtured the idea that he would return to the Chinese mainland, 172-173

Clark, Captain Joseph J., USN (USNA, 1917)
Commanded the carrier Yorktown (CV-10) during the invasion of the Gilbert Islands in November 1943, 43, 47; did not make a rendezvous for an attack on Truk in 1944 because of a communications error, 56-57

Communications
One of the few times Rear Admiral Marc Mitscher was angry came in 1944 when a communicator put the wrong precedence on a message concerning a planned attack on Truk, 56-57; problem with padding in a radio message from Admiral Chester Nimitz to Admiral William Halsey during the Battle of Leyte Gulf in October 1944, 97-98

Delco-Remy
As a division of the General Motors Corporation, it was involved in manufacturing items for the Department of Defense in the 1950s and 1960s, 197-212

Dewey, Admiral of the Navy George, USN (USNA, 1858)
The roll-top desk he used as head of the Navy's General Board early in the century was still around in Main Navy in 1947, 159-162

Duncan, Captain Donald B., USN (USNA, 1917)
As prospective commanding officer of the carrier Essex (CV-9) in 1942, received regular progress briefings from Hedding, the executive officer, 32-33, 35

Education
   Relatively primitive in New Mexico in the 1910s, 1-2;
   curriculum at the Naval Academy in the early 1920s, 3;
   postgraduate studies in aeronautical engineer in
   Annapolis and at MIT, 1929-31, 8-11

Ekstrom, Lieutenant (junior grade) Clarence E., USN (USNA, 1924)
   In the late 1920s became one of the U.S. first naval
   aviators to take postgraduate education in aeronautical
   engineering, 10

Essex, USS (CV-9)
   As the first of her class, she was not really complete
   when she went in commission in December 1942, 32;
   replacement of unsatisfactory officers, 32-33;
   preparation of the ship for war service, 33-36

Far East Command, U.S.
   In the early 1950s responsibility for such areas as
   Taiwan and the Philippines were moved from the Far East
   Command to the Pacific Command, 170-172

Fighting Squadron Two (VF-2)
   Had cream-of-the-crop enlisted pilots flying as wingmen
   to the officers in the late 1930s, 26-27; Hedding once
   landed over the bow of the carrier Lexington (CV-2),
   34-35

Formosa
   See Taiwan

Formosa Patrol Force
   Operated reconnaissance patrols out of the Pescadores,
   Philippines, and Okinawa in the mid-1950s, 176-178

Fuchida, Captain Mitsuo, IJN
   Japanese aviator who was interviewed about kamikaze
   pilots by the strategic bombing survey after World War
   II, 116-117, 153

Forrestal, James V.
   As Secretary of the Navy in 1947, directed the General
   Board to review the Navy's shore establishment, with an
   eye toward reducing it in scope, 160-162

General Board, U.S. Navy
   Role of in 1947 in assessing the Navy's shore
   establishment, 158-162; Admiral John Towers as chairman
   in 1947, 159-160; Captain Hedding inherited a desk once
   used by Admiral George Dewey, 159-160; composition of in
   1947, 161

General Motors Corporation
   Involvement in contracting with the Department of Defense
   in the 1950s and 1960s, 197-212

Gilbert Islands
In 1943, during the Tarawa invasion, the fast carriers got away from the previous rigid restrictions on procedures for refueling at sea, 39-40; planning for the invasion of the Gilberts in November 1943, 43-45; support by U.S. carrier aircraft, 45-47

Ginder, Rear Admiral Samuel P., USN (USNA, 1916)
Sometimes acted irrationally as Commander Task Group 58.3 in the spring of 1944, 67-70; relieved of command, 70

Gingrich, Rear Admiral John E., USN (USNA, 1920)
Was chief of staff when the Pacific Command became truly joint in the early 1950s, 169-170

Guadalcanal
Postwar interrogation of the chief of staff to Vice Gunichi Mikawa during the August 1942 Battle of Savo Island, 148-149

Guam
Staging base for Japanese aircraft during the U.S. invasion of the Marianas in June 1944, 76-77; Fleet Admiral Chester Nimitz's Pacific Fleet headquarters moved from Hawaii to Guam in January 1945, 106-108; cheap whiskey was available at the naval officers' club in the summer of 1945, 128-129

Gunnery--Naval
Effective antiaircraft fire by U.S. 5-inch projectiles equipped with proximity fuzes during a carrier strike against the Marianas Islands in February 1944, 54

Halsey, Admiral William F., Jr., USN (USNA, 1904)
Role in the controversial Battle of Leyte Gulf in October 1944, 96-102, 151; was blamed for the damage to Third Fleet ships when they ran into typhoons in December 1944 and June 1945, 103-105

Hawaii
Only one hotel was on Oahu's Waikiki Beach when the U.S. Fleet visited in 1925, 4-5; VF-6 conducted a surprise mock attack on Hawaii in the early 1930s, 14-16

See also Pearl Harbor, Kahului Naval Air Station

Heath, Captain John P., USN (USNA, 1921)
As a detail officer in the Bureau of Aeronautics in the summer of 1945, he helped get Hedding reassigned from an aircraft carrier to the strategic bombing survey, 126-127

Hedding, Vice Admiral Truman, J., USN (Ret.) (USNA, 1924)
Boyhood in Pennsylvania and New Mexico, 1-2; parents of, 1-2; education of, 1-2; appointment to the Naval Academy, 2-3; experiences as a midshipman, 1920-24, 3; served in

the battleship Maryland (BB-46), 1924-25, 4-6; flight
training at Pensacola, Florida, 1925-26, 6-7; duty in
Fighting Squadron One, 1927-29, 7-8; postgraduate school,
1929-31, 8-11; flight test at Anacostia, 1931-32, 11-12;
duty in the carrier Saratoga (CV-3), 1932-33, 12-14;
Fighting Squadron Six, 1933-35, 14-16; duty in the Bureau
of Aeronautics, 1935-37, 17-20; as an assistant naval
aide in the White House, 1936-37, 20-25; duty as exec and
commanding officer of VF-2, 1937-40, 26-27; duty from
1940 to 1942 at Pensacola Naval Air Station, 27-31;
served in the commissioning crew of the carrier Essex
(CV-9) in 1942-43, 31-36; chief of staff to Commander
Carrier Division Three, 1943-44, 36-67, 72-86; temporary
chief of staff to Rear Admiral Samuel Ginder in 1944,
67-70; temporary duty with Admiral Raymond Spruance's
staff to plan for the invasion of the Marianas in 1944,
87-89; was a member of Admiral Chester Nimitz's Pacific
Fleet planning staff in 1944-45, 89-126; service shortly
after the end of World War II as a member of the
strategic bombing survey in Japan, 127-157; commanded the
naval air station at Kahului, Maui, Hawaii, in 1946-47,
154, 157-158; brief service on the Navy's General Board
in 1947, 158-162; student at the National War College in
1947-48, 162-164; commanded the aircraft carrier Valley
Forge (CV-45) in 1948-49, 164-165; served on the Joint
Staff, 1949-51, 165-168; served on the staff of Commander
in Chief Pacific from 1951 to 1953, 168-175; Commanded
the Formosa Patrol Force, 1953-54, 175-178; service on
the Joint Staff, 1954-55, 179-188; as special assistant
to the JCS chairman, 1955-56, 188-195; commanded Carrier
Division Three, 1956-57, 194-195; served as Bureau of
Aeronautics representative in the western district,
1957-58, 195-196; employment with Delco-Remy and General
Motors following Navy retirement in 1959, 196-212;
activities after retirement from GM in 1965, 212-213

Hirohito, Emperor
Japanese Emperor's role in his nation's decision to
surrender in 1945 and end World War II, 144-145

Inter-Service Rivalry
Competition for funds among the various U.S. armed
services in the early 1950s, 181-182, 185-187, 194

Iwo Jima
Pacific island on which Japanese emerged from caves in
the spring of 1945 and killed some American pilots after
the island was supposedly secure, 93-94

Japan
U.S. planning for the possible invasion of Japan in 1945-
46, 109-111; ramifications of the U.S. use of atomic
bombs against Japanese cities in August 1945, 111-114;
Marquis Kido, Lord Keeper of the Privy Seal, was
interrogated shortly after World War II by the U.S.
Strategic Bombing Survey concerning the steps leading up

to the Japanese surrender in August 1945, 111-113, 142-143; Major General Curtis E. LeMay of the Army Air Forces directed the tactics used in B-29 bombing raids against Japan in the spring and summer of 1945, 120-121; in 1945 Major General Curtis LeMay declined to run bombing campaigns against Japan in coordination with Navy carrier planes, 121-123; Pacific Fleet staff planning for the intended invasion of Japan in 1945-46, 123-124; officers of the U.S. Strategic Bombing Survey worked in Tokyo shortly after the end of World War II to conduct interrogations, 129-131; evaluation of the role of conventional and atomic bombs in the campaign against Japan, 132-133, 138; decision to go to war in 1941, 143-144; decision to surrender in 1945, 144-145

See also Strategic Bombing Survey, U.S.

Japanese Army
Role at the beginning and end of World War II, 143-144

Japanese Navy
Suicide attack on the carrier Randolph (CV-15) at Ulithi in March 1945, 60; in the Battle of the Philippine Sea in June 1944, 76-79; role during the Battle of Leyte Gulf in October 1944, 96-102, 151-152; kamikaze attacks against U.S. ships involved in the Okinawa operation in the spring of 1945, 115-118, 153; questioning of Japanese naval officers at the war college near Tokyo shortly after the end of World War II as part of the U.S. Strategic Bombing Survey, 133-136, 139-140, 148-153; stored wartime action reports in caves on northern Honshu, 139-140; the battleship Yamato made a suicidal voyage from Japan to Okinawa in April 1945 and was sunk by U.S. carrier planes, 140-141; in the Battle of Savo Island at Guadalcanal in August 1942, 148-149; discussion of the sinking of the carrier Shinano in November 1944, 156-157

Joint Staff, Joint Chiefs of Staff
In the 1949-51 period, the staff's strategic planning group worked on a variety of issues, including the possible use of nuclear weapons, 165-167; Air Force members of the staff were well organized in terms of the service's party line on various issues, 167-168; in the mid-1950s the Strategic Planning Group was charged with developing plans for both near and long term, 180-183, 193; competition for funds among the various armed services in the early 1950s, 181-182, 185-187, 194; conflicts in planning papers forwarded to the Joint Chiefs, 183-187; composition in mid-1950s, 191-192

Kahului Naval Air Station, Maui, Hawaii
Captain's quarters and officers' club damaged by tidal wave in April 1946, 157-158

Kamikazes
   Suicide attack on the carrier Randolph (CV-15) at Ulithi in March 1945, 60; attacks against U.S. ships involved in the Okinawa operation in the spring of 1945, 115-118, 153; in the Philippines in late 1944, 153; use of baka bombs attached to mother planes, 154

Kido, Marquis
   Japanese Lord Keeper of the Privy Seal, he was interrogated shortly after World War II by the U.S. Strategic Bombing Survey concerning the steps leading up to the Japanese surrender, 111-113, 142-144

King, Admiral Ernest J., USN (USNA, 1901)
   Worked hard and played hard as Chief of the Bureau of Aeronautics in the mid-1930s, 17; requested Hedding as his flag lieutenant in 1939, 17-19; promised President Roosevelt that the carrier Essex (CV-9) would go into commission in 1942, and she did, 32; in the spring of 1944 specified that aviation admirals have surface officers as chiefs of staff, 62-63; as a member of the Joint Chiefs of Staff in World War II, helped formulate plans to be executed by lower echelons of command, 90

Konoye, Prince
   Former Japanese Prime Minister who killed himself in December 1945, shortly after being interviewed by the U.S. Strategic Bombing Survey, 141-142

Kurita, Vice Admiral Takeo, IJN
   Postwar interrogation concerning his role during the Battle of Leyte Gulf in October 1944, 98-99, 149-152

Kwajalein Atoll
   Air strike against in December 1943 by U.S. carrier planes, 48-49

LeMay, Major General Curtis E., USA
   Army Air Forces officer who directed the tactics used in B-29 bombing raids against Japan in the spring and summer of 1945, 120-121; in early 1945 declined to run coordinated bombing campaigns against Japan in coordination with Navy carrier planes, 121-123

Lexington, USS (CV-2)
   Hedding landed over the bow when the ship was operating off Hawaii in the late 1930s, 34-35

Lexington, USS (CV-16)
   Rear Admiral Marc Mitscher's flagship while serving as commander of the fast carrier task force in the spring of 1944, 65, 84

Leyte Gulf, Battle of
   Monitoring of this October 1944 battle by the Pacific

Fleet staff in Hawaii, 96-102; postwar interrogations of the Japanese concerning the battle, 98-99, 149-152

MacArthur, General Douglas, USA (USMA, 1903)
Work in 1944-45 in planning future operations in conjunction with Admiral Chester Nimitz and the Pacific Fleet, 92-93, 106; arrival in Japan after the surrender in September 1945, 114

Majuro Atoll
Rear Admiral Marc Mitscher and Hedding went for a ride in a cruiser floatplane in order to get their necessary flight time while they were at Majuro in 1944, 58-59; as a fleet recreation site, 59

Marianas Islands
U.S. carrier air strike against in February 1944, 53; carrier operations in support of the invasion in June 1944, 75-82; role of Hedding in providing carrier planning for the support of the invasion, 87-89

Marshall Islands
Air strike against Kwajalein in December 1943 by U.S. carrier planes, 48-49; pre-invasion bombardment in January 1944, 52-53; Rear Admiral Marc Mitscher and Hedding went for a ride in a cruiser floatplane in order to get their necessary flight time while they were at Majuro in 1944, 58-59; Majuro as a fleet recreation site, 59

Maryland, USS (BB-46)
Made an eventful cruise from the West Coast to Hawaii and Australia in 1925, 4-6; aviators on board, 6

Massachusetts Institute of Technology, Cambridge
Provided a strenuous course in aeronautical engineering in the early 1930s, 9-11

McCain, Vice Admiral John S., USN (USNA, 1906)
During the Battle of Leyte Gulf in October 1944, he was in command of a carrier task group headed for Ulithi when he learned of a Japanese force in San Bernardino Strait, 151

McMorris, Vice Admiral Charles H., USN (USNA, 1912)
Served as a balance wheel on Admiral Chester Nimitz's Pacific Fleet staff during World War II, 90-92; hesitant in 1945 about letting Hedding leave the staff to command an aircraft carrier, 124-125

Mikawa, Vice Admiral Gunichi, IJN
Role in the Battle of Savo Island at Guadalcanal in August 1942, 148-149

Mitscher, Rear Admiral Marc A., USN (USNA, 1910)
Took command of Carrier Division Three and the fast

carrier task force in January 1944, 52; directed the
carrier strike against the Marianas Islands in February
1944, 53-54; as executive officer of the carrier Saratoga
(CV-3) in the early 1930s, he relied on his subordinates
more than had his predecessor, Commander Richmond Kelly
Turner, 54-55; kindness as a person, 55, 57; rare case of
anger when a communication officer made a mistake
concerning a raid on Truk, 56-57; went for an airplane
ride at Majuro Atoll in 1944 in order to get his
necessary flight time, 58-59; reaction to receiving a
surface officer, Captain Arleigh Burke, as chief of staff
in the spring of 1944, 62-67, 83-86; role in command of
Task Force 58 during the Marianas invasion in June 1944,
75-82

Montgomery, Rear Admiral Alfred E., USN (USNA, 1912)
Was cautious about conducting a fighter sweep in
connection with an air strike on Kwajalein in December
1943, 48-51

Moore, Brigadier General Ernest C., USA
Received presents from Navy men Hedding and Forrest
Sherman when they visited his Seventh Fighter Command on
the island of Iwo Jima in early 1945, 93-94

National War College, Washington, D.C.
Foreign students left after the 1947-48 school year
because of U.S. concerns about compromise of classified
information, 163; students included many flag and general
officers, 164

Naval Academy, U.S., Annapolis, Maryland
Curriculum in the early 1920s, 3

Newport News Shipbuilding and Dry Dock Company
Construction of the carrier Essex (CV-9), which was
commissioned in December 1942, 31-35

Nichol, Lieutenant Commander Bromfield B., USN (USNA, 1924)
Was in the back seat of an SBD carrying a message to
Admiral Husband Kimmel when it was shot at by the
Japanese during the 1941 attack on Pearl Harbor, 30-31

Night Flying
Lieutenant Commander Edward H. O'Hare was shot down by
accident during a night tactical experiment in November
1943, 47-48

Nimitz, Admiral Chester W., USN (USNA, 1905)
In 1943 he directed the development of tactical doctrine
for the fast carrier task force, 37-40; planning for the
invasion of the Gilbert Islands in November 1943, 43-45;
directed an air strike against Kwajalein in December
1943, 48-49; kindness as a person, 55; ordered carrier
strikes on Truk in 1944, 56-57, 61-62; in early 1944
relayed a message to Rear Admiral Marc Mitscher directing

that he have a surface officer as chief of staff, 62; makeup of Pacific Fleet planning staff in 1944, 89-92; staff monitoring of the Battle of Leyte Gulf in October 1944, 96-102; relationship with the closest members of his staff, 102-103; reaction to the Third Fleet's encounter with a typhoon in December 1944, 103-105; desired personal contact with subordinate commanders, 106; moved the Pacific Fleet headquarters to Guam in January 1945, 106-108; enjoyed meeting fellow Texans, 123; received a message on 10 August 1945 about impending Japanese surrender, 125-126

Nitze, Paul H.
Headed the U.S. Strategic Bombing Survey, which interrogated Japanese leaders in 1945, following the end of World War II, 131, 137

Nuclear Weapons
Ramifications of the U.S. use of atomic bombs against Japanese cities in August 1945, 111-114; evaluation of the role of atomic bombs in the campaign against Japan, 132-133; the strategic planning group of the Joint Staff dealt in 1949-51 with potential uses of nuclear weapons, 165-167

Oakland, USS (CL-95)
Futile role in support of night air operations of Kwajalein in December 1943, 50

Ofstie, Rear Admiral Ralph A., USN (USNA, 1919)
Headed the Navy section of the U.S. Strategic Bombing Survey that interrogated Japanese leaders shortly after the conclusion of World War II, 127-128, 136-138, 149

O'Hare, Lieutenant Commander Edward H., USN (USNA, 1937)
Shot down by accident during a night tactical experiment in November 1943, 47-48

Ohmae, Captain Toshikazu, IJN
Japanese naval officer who provided information to U.S. Navy interrogators shortly after the end of World War II, 134-136, 148-149

Okinawa
Kamikaze attacks against U.S. ships involved in the Okinawa operation in the spring of 1945, 115-118; description of conditions when Hedding and Rear Admiral Forrest Sherman visited in the spring of 1945, 119-120

Onishi, Vice Admiral Takijiro, IJN
Founder of the Japanese kamikaze corps, he committed suicide right at the end of World War II, 117-118

Ostrander, Lieutenant Commander John E., USN (USNA, 1917)
Served as a naval aide in the White House in the late 1930s, 20

Ozawa, Vice Admiral Jisaburo, IJN
Role during the Battle of Leyte Gulf in October 1944, 102

Pacific Command, U.S.
In the early 1950s, the command became truly joint, rather than being just the Pacific Fleet, 169-170; in the early 1950s received responsibility for Taiwan and the Philippines, both previously under General Douglas MacArthur, 170-172; in the mid-1950s, CinCPac was split off as a completely separate command from Pacific Fleet, 174-175

Pacific Fleet, U.S.
Makeup of fleet planning staff in 1944, 89-92; staff monitoring of the Battle of Leyte Gulf in October 1944, 96-102; headquarters moved to Guam in January 1945, 106-108; planning for the possible invasion of Japan in 1945-46, 109-111; Pacific Fleet staff planning for the intended invasion of Japan in 1945-46, 123-124

Palau Islands
Struck by a raid from the U.S. fast carrier task force in the spring of 1944, 64-65, 71

Paria, Gulf of
The carrier Essex (CV-9) did her shakedown training here, off the coast of Venezuela, in 1943, 35

Pearl Harbor
Precautions taken at the Pensacola Naval Air Station in response to the 1941 Japanese attack at Pearl Harbor, 28-29; when Japanese leaders were interrogated after World War II, they said they had had no intention of invading Hawaii, only attacking the fleet, 29-30; the Japanese shot at an SBD that was carrying a message to Admiral Husband Kimmel at the time of the attack, 30-31

Pensacola Naval Air Station
Precautions taken at the air station in response to the Japanese attack on Pearl Harbor in 1941, 28-29; expansion after the war started, 31

Philippine Islands
In the early 1950s the Joint Chiefs of Staff transferred responsibility for the Philippines to the Pacific Command from General Douglas MacArthur, 170-172

Planning
Preparations for the invasion of the Gilbert Islands in November 1943, 43-45; role of Hedding in providing carrier planning for the support of the Marianas invasion in 1944, 87-89; makeup of Pacific Fleet planning staff in 1944, 89-92; planning for the possible invasion of Japan in 1945-46, 109-111; in 1945 Major General Curtis LeMay declined to run bombing campaigns against Japan in

coordination with Navy carrier planes, 121-123; Pacific Fleet staff planning for the intended invasion of Japan in 1945-46, 123-124; the strategic planning group of the Joint Staff dealt in 1949-51 with potential uses of nuclear weapons, 165-167; in the mid-1950s the Strategic Planning Group was charged with developing plans for both near and long term, 180-183, 193; conflicts in planning papers forwarded to the Joint Chiefs, 183-187

Pownall, Rear Admiral Charles A., USN (USNA, 1910)
As Commander Carrier Division Three in 1943, was head of a board to develop tactical doctrine for the fast carrier task force, 36-40; strikes against Wake and Marcus islands in late 1943, 41-42; was cautious about conducting a fighter sweep in connection with an air strike on Kwajalein in December 1943, 48-50; relieved as commander of the fast carrier task force in late 1943 because of a perception that he wasn't aggressive enough, 50-52

Radford, Admiral Arthur W., USN (USNA, 1916)
In the early 1950s Radford was commander in chief when the Pacific Command became a joint operation, 169-172; frustration as Chairman of the Joint Chiefs in the mid-1950s when confronted with conflicts from the joint planning committee, 184-185, 190-191; rundown of individuals on his personal staff, 189; responsibilities, 189-190

Randolph, USS (CV-15)
Attacked by a Japanese kamikaze while the crew was watching movies in March 1945, 60

Read, Captain Albert C., USN (USNA, 1907)
Was commanding officer of the naval air station at Pensacola when World War II began and directed its expansion, 28, 31

Reeves, Rear Admiral Joseph M., USN (USNA, 1894)
Pushed aircraft carrier tactics in the U.S. Fleet in the early 1930s, 15-16; student of naval history, 16

Refueling
In 1943, at Hedding's suggestion, the fast carriers got away from the previous rigid restrictions on procedures for refueling at sea, 39-40

Roosevelt, Mrs. Eleanor
Role of naval aides when she was involved in White House social functions in the mid-1930s, 21-24; kindness toward Hedding in 1936, 23-24

Roosevelt, President Franklin D.
Role of naval aides when he was involved in White House social functions in the mid-1930s, 21-25; was promised by Admiral Ernest J. King that the carrier Essex (CV-9)

would go into commission in 1942, 32

Royal Navy
Presented an award to Fleet Admiral Chester Nimitz on 10 August 1945, shortly before the Japanese surrender, 125-126

Saratoga, USS (CV-3)
Role of the landing signal officer in the early 1930s, 12-14; mock attacks on Pearl Harbor and the Panama Canal in the early 1930s, 14-15; as executive officer in the early 1930s, Commander Marc Mitscher relied on his subordinates more than had his predecessor, Commander Richmond Kelly Turner, 54-55

Savo Island, Battle of
Postwar interrogation of the officer who was chief of staff to Vice Admiral Gunichi Mikawa during this battle in August 1942, 148-149

Security
Foreign students were dropped from the National War College after the 1947-48 school year because of U.S. concerns about compromise of classified information, 163

Seversky, Major Alexander de, USAR
An exponent of air power, he made speeches while interrogating the Japanese after World War II, 146-147

Sherman, Rear Admiral Forrest P., USN (USNA, 1918)
Role on Admiral Chester Nimitz's Pacific Fleet planning staff in 1944, 90-95; sent Hedding to Ulithi in late 1944 with the plans for the Third Fleet after the Leyte operation, 95; wrote a dispatch to Admiral William Halsey in the Battle of Leyte Gulf in October 1944, 97

Shinano (Japanese Aircraft Carrier)
Discussion during the postwar Strategic Bombing Survey of the sinking of the ship by the submarine Archerfish (SS-311) in November 1944, 156-157

Shore Establishment, U.S. Navy
As Secretary of the Navy in 1947, James Forrestal directed the General Board to review the Navy's shore establishment, with an eye toward reducing it in scope, 160-162

Spruance, Vice Admiral Raymond A., USN (USNA, 1907)
As Commander Fifth Fleet in February 1944, led a strike against Truk, 62; wanted battleships to sink the Japanese Yamato the following year, 62; received an aviator as chief of staff in the spring of 1944, 63, role in command of the Marianas invasion in June 1944, 75-82; Hedding provided planning help for the invasion of the Marianas in June 1944 because Spruance's staff did not have a strong aviator, 87-89; frustrated in his hope to get

American battleships into action against the Japanese battleship Yamato in April 1945, 140-141

Strategic Bombing Survey, U.S.
When Japanese leaders were interrogated after World War II, they said they had had no intention of invading Hawaii, only attacking the fleet, 29-30; During the interrogation, explanations for Vice Admiral Takeo Kurita's role in the Battle of Leyte Gulf in October 1944, 99, 149-152; Vice Admiral Jisaburo Ozawa's explanation of his role at Leyte, 102; interrogation of Japanese leaders concerning the impact of the use of atomic bombs against Japan in August 1945, 111-114, 132-133, 138, 144-145; coverage of the Okinawa campaign and kamikazes, 115-118, 153; personnel in leadership positions during the survey, 127-129; questioning of Japanese naval officers at the war college near Tokyo shortly after the end of World War II, 133-136, 139-140, 148-149; Prince Konoye, former Japanese Prime Minister, killed himself in December 1945, shortly after being interviewed, 141-142; Japanese decision to surrender in 1945, 144-145; during the interrogations the Army Air Forces made inflated claims on behalf of its bombing effectiveness in World War II, 145-147; language difficulties sometimes created problems relating answers to questions, 146; discussion of the sinking of the carrier Shinano in November 1944, 156-157

TBF Avenger
A TBF apparently shot down Lieutenant Commander Edward H. O'Hare during night tactical experiments in November 1943, 47-48

Tactics
Development of tactical doctrine in 1943 for the fast carrier task force, 37-40; Major General Curtis E. LeMay of the Army Air Forces directed the tactics used in B-29 bombing raids against Japan in the spring and summer of 1945, 120-121

Taiwan
In the early 1950s the Joint Chiefs of Staff transferred responsibility for Taiwan to the Pacific Command from General Douglas MacArthur, 170-172; in the early 1950s Generalissimo Chiang Kai-shek nurtured the idea that his Chinese nationalists would return to the mainland, 172-173; William C. Bullitt was an anti-Semitic, anti-Communist individual who served as U.S. ambassador to Taiwan in the early 1950s, 173

Task Force 58
Rear Admiral Marc Mitscher became the new commander in January 1944, 52; strike against the Marianas Islands in February 1944, 53; pre-invasion strike on the Marshall Islands in January 1944, 52-53; attacks on Truk in early 1944, 56-57, 61-62; Commodore Arleigh Burke became chief

of staff to Vice Admiral Marc Mitscher in the spring of 1944, although Mitscher was initially reluctant to have him, 63-67, 83-86; strikes against the Palau Islands in the spring of 1944, 64-65, 71; Rear Admiral Samuel P. Ginder sometimes acted irrationally as Commander Task Group 58.3 in the spring of 1944 and had to be relieved, 67-70; carrier operations in support of the Marianas invasion in June 1944, 75-82

Tokyo, Japan
Officers of the U.S. Strategic Bombing Survey worked in Tokyo shortly after the end of World War II to conduct interrogations, 129-131

Towers, Admiral John H., USN (USNA, 1906)
Expressed concern in 1944 because some staff commanded by surface officers did not have sufficient expertise about naval aviation, 88; as chairman of the Navy's General Board during part of 1947, 159-160

Toyoda, Admiral Soemu, IJN
During post-World War II interrogation provided explanation for Vice Admiral Takeo Kurita's role in the Battle of Leyte Gulf in October 1944, 99; questioned after the war about the Japanese decision to surrender in August 1945, 113-114, 144-145

Truk, Caroline Islands
One of the few times Rear Admiral Marc Mitscher was angry came in 1944 when a communicator put the wrong precedence on a message concerning a planned attack on Truk, 56-57; carrier strike in February 1944, 61-62

Turner, Commander Richmond K., USN (USNA, 1908)
Duty as executive officer of the carrier Saratoga (CV-3) in the early 1930s, 12, 54-55

Typhoons
Fleet Admiral Chester Nimitz's reaction to the storms that damaged the Third Fleet in December 1944 and June 1945, 103-105

Ulithi Atoll, Caroline Islands
Role as a fleet anchorage and recreation base in 1944-45, 59-60; kamikaze attack on the carrier Randolph (CV-15) in March 1945, 60

Uniforms
Even though he was a naval officer, Captain Truman Hedding wore an Army uniform while participating in the U.S. Strategic Bombing Survey in Japan in 1945, 146

Van Valkenburgh, Lieutenant Commander Franklin, USN (USNA, 1909)
Relied a great deal on Hedding's help while serving as navigator of the battleship Maryland in 1925, 5

Weather
  Fleet Admiral Chester Nimitz's reaction to the typhoons that damaged the Third Fleet in December 1944 and June 1945, 103-105; in April 1946 a tidal wave damaged the captain's quarters and officers' club at Kahului Naval Air Station, Maui, Hawaii, 157-158

White House, Washington, D.C.
  Social role of assistant naval aides to President Franklin D. Roosevelt in the mid-1930s, 20-25

Yamamoto, Admiral Isoroku, IJN
  Involvement in the Japanese decision to go to war in late 1941, 143-144

Yamato (Japanese Battleship)
  Made a suicidal voyage from Japan to Okinawa in April 1945 and was sunk by U.S. carrier planes, 140-141

Yorktown, USS (CV-10)
  Commanded by Captain Jocko Clark during the invasion of the Gilbert Islands in November 1943, 43, 47

www.ingramcontent.com/pod-product-compliance
Lightning Source LLC
Chambersburg PA
CBHW080614170426
43209CB00007B/1429